I'LL HAVE WHAT SHE'S HAVING

SIMPLICITY: DESIGN, TECHNOLOGY, BUSINESS, LIFE
John Maeda, Editor

The Laws of Simplicity, John Maeda, 2006

The Plenitude: Creativity, Innovation, and Making Stuff, Rich Gold, 2007

Simulation and Its Discontents, Sherry Turkle, 2009

Redesigning Leadership, John Maeda, 2011

I'll Have What She's Having: Mapping Social Behavior, Alex Bentley, Mark Earls, and Michael J. O'Brien, 2011

I'LL HAVE WHAT SHE'S HAVING

Mapping Social Behavior

ALEX BENTLEY, MARK EARLS, AND MICHAEL J. O'BRIEN

The MIT Press
Cambridge, Massachusetts
London, England

This book was set in Scala and Scala Sans by the MIT Press.

Library of Congress Cataloging-in-Publication Data

I'll have what she's having : mapping social behavior / Alex Bentley, Mark Earls, and
Michael J. O'Brien ; foreword by John Maeda.

   p.   cm. — (Simplicity: design, technology, business, life)

Includes bibliographical references and index.

ISBN 978-0-262-01615-5 (hbk. : alk. paper), 978-0-262-55380-3 (pb)

1. Social learning. 2. Social interaction. 3. Social psychology. I. Bentley, Alex,
1970– II. Earls, Mark. III. O'Brien, Michael J. (Michael John), 1950–

HM1106.I42 2011   303.3'2—dc22   2011004966

149836348

CONTENTS

CONTENTS

FOREWORD

John Maeda

Simplicity is a desirable state to achieve in the complex world we live in today, especially with the ongoing turmoil in our world's economy. Alex Bentley, Mark Earls, and Michael O'Brien's assertion that our civilization's guaranteed means for survival has always been quite simple—namely to just copy the other guy—is an important one. It means that we need not worry at all because someone out there is bound to come up with a solution. And we will all copy it en masse.

But what does their work say for all manners of copying? For example, in the negative forms of copying that we know, such as academic plagiarism or copyright infringement, we exact a serious punishment on such instances of "diffusion of innovation"—to use the authors' terms. In our inherently social environment rooted in the desire to achieve fairness and justice, we prescribe judgment on what makes a certain kind of innovation appropriate—and thus, make it more complex for innovation and much of the "social learning" described in this book to happen.

The work described in this book will make you scratch your head and wonder about your own culture's proclivities for sharing (or hoarding)—whether that be your culture at work, your country's, or the unique social space within your own family. If innovation is, as the authors imply in this text, just one part good idea and many other parts setting it loose to be copied, then you will think differently about how tightly you hold onto "your stuff" and increase your own inclination to just let it all go. Doesn't that feel simple? Now, just don't tell your intellectual property lawyer (smile).

PREFACE: IN KATZ'S DELI

Much of the 1989 Rob Reiner movie *When Harry Met Sally* now seems more than a little sugary. This tale of dating and friendship among Manhattan's middle class trumpets its moral almost as loudly as its plot twists, as Harry (Billy Crystal) and Sally (Meg Ryan) meet and mate and remeet (as friends) and so on, until the inevitable final reunion. That said, the movie contains one of the more memorable scenes of romantic comedy. As they're sitting in a Lower East Side delicatessen, the topic of female orgasms comes up, and Harry tells Sally that no woman has ever faked one with him. How does he know? Sally asks. He just knows, Harry responds. Sally then shows him—and the rest of the deli's clientele—just how wrong he is.

What happens after that is what lies at the heart of our book. At the next table is a woman of what is politely known as "a certain age," who says to the waiter, "I'll have what she's having." Such a simple phrase, and yet "What she's having" signifies humankind's amazing ability for social learning. We learn from those around us, from those around those around us, and on outward, both in time and space, to people whom we'll never meet and people long dead. "What she's having" is what this book is all about: how social learning shapes human behavior at multiple levels, from individuals to communities to populations. Without grasping the importance of "What she's having," no map of human behavior is complete.

We are certainly not the first to publish a book on human behavior. From Gabriele Tarde's *The Laws of Imitation* in the nineteenth century and Dale Carnegie's *How to Win Friends and Influence People* of the 1930s, to Malcolm Gladwell's *The Tipping Point* and Richard Thaler and Cass Sunstein's *Nudge*, our thirst for science about ourselves is insatiable. We can't get enough of easily digested information about why we do the things we do. Politicians, policymakers, and business leaders are particularly keen on getting us to behave the way they want us to.

Wherever we seek to shape behavior, it's become clear just how difficult it is to bring about change. For every widely adopted piece of shiny technology such as the iPod, most marketing campaigns fail to attract even modest attention. Corporations usually fail to change their employees' behavior, and democratic governments usually fail to change citizens' behavior. Of the billions of dollars of our (retirement) money spent on mergers and acquisitions, most reduce shareholder value as mutually hostile employees fail to deliver the promised synergies. Many of the challenges we face, from the fallout of the global financial crisis to combating climate change, are as much social as they are technological: we need a better map of how collective human behavior works.

Part of our myopia is inherited from the Enlightenment and classical economic theory, epitomized by the "rational-choice" model, often more wishful gospel than empirical truth. The central thrust of the new "behavioral economics" so beloved by politicians is that we are far from being rational agents who think and act according to what we calculate to be in our own best interests. Most of the time we make mistakes and act in surprisingly irrational ways. Our minds are full of biases and errors, and our thinking is lazy and shorthanded—when we can be bothered to think at all.

Behavioral economics has improved the map in important ways. So has evolutionary psychology, a discipline that explores how human brains, biologically adapted to a very different Pleistocene world, cope with the one we live in today. This explains a few things. Half an hour on New York's gridlocked streets or in a London pub will show just how our "caveman" roots can surface. Likewise, our bodies are bloated from the glut of sweet and fatty foods our ancestors were bound to seek out.

But neither of these two corrective projects, behavioral economics or evolutionary psychology, goes far enough. Both avoid the obvious fact that humans are, first and foremost, social creatures. Yes, we can be lazy thinkers, and yes, we have Pleistocene brains, but a large part of our success during the Pleistocene and since then is attributable to our doing what we do with those around us, to learn from and influence each other so naturally that we hardly notice it. We use the brains of others to think for us and as a place to store knowledge about the world; almost everything we know and do involves shared knowledge from past and present people—billions of them by now. To understand human behavior, we need to move from the "me" perspective to the "we" perspective.

Why does any of this matter? Philosophically, it matters because—as Steven Pinker argued in *Blank Slate*—working from false assumptions about people is bad for business and politics and bad for scholarship. Practically, it matters because our social inheritance underlies modern human life in a huge, increasingly interconnected population of people to learn from, and an enormous oversupply of choices in our lives.

Four centuries ago, amateur astronomers changed forever how we saw the cosmos and our place within it. We believe that something similar is happening with the current explosion of research on human social influence and cultural evolution, fueled by the widespread popularity of "social" connective media such as phones, social-networking platforms, and the Internet as a whole. This book attempts to describe a new map of human behavior that pulls together this learning. To build it, we present experimental and real-world examples and adopt different perspectives, depending on the issue. We zoom out from the individual in a box who does a few tricks, to people influencing each other in pairs or in small social groups, to the behavioral complexities characteristic of larger groups. As we move up in scale, we consider ideas, behavior, and social practices. We use the notion of different landscapes for cultural evolution, starting with assumptions about individuals in more predictable, smooth, and static social landscapes and then moving on to populations in more rugged, unpredictable, and dynamic social landscapes. But all the time, our map encompasses the ability of our species to learn from its peers: to "have what she's [or he's] having."

This is far more than a descriptive or theoretical exercise. Our ambition is to provide you with a practical and usable map to help you navigate your way through the complex world of human behavior and—if your ambition is to change it—to do so with greater hope of success. Some of what we have to say will be familiar to social scientists, but we've tried to present a new and practical synthesis, while expressing our appreciation along the way for the sheer elegance and impact of the subject.

We take this opportunity to thank Bob Prior, executive editor of the MIT Press, for his unflagging support of the project. In fact, Bob was the person who first suggested we write this book. We also thank John Maeda, editor of the Design, Technology, Business, Life series published by the MIT Press. His book *The Laws of Simplicity* not only was an inspiration for us but also provided an excellent guide for how to focus and present our discussion. Finally, we thank Melody Galen for producing the figures, Susan Buckley of the MIT Press for providing excellent editorial suggestions, and the Leverhulme Trust for funding the Tipping Points project at Durham University, which sparked some of our collective interests.

OUT OF THE TREES

The writer and critic Susan Sontag once suggested that science fiction is not really about science at all. Hardcore sci-fi author Philip K. Dick pointed to the roots of the genre in seventeenth-century travel and adventure stories. Our feeling is that Arthur C. Clarke was perhaps nearer the mark when he supposedly suggested that science fiction is really just about us and, more particularly, about our ideas about ourselves. Certainly one of the most influential sci-fi works, Gene Roddenberry's *Star Trek* series, is, just as its creator intended, part *Wagon Train* to the stars and part human morality tale.

At the heart of every *Star Trek* story lie deep and troubling questions about what it is to be human. In the original television series, this is often dramatized through interactions between the *Enterprise* crew members and various alien life forms they meet as they "boldly go" to the unknown reaches of the universe. Episodes also show struggles between the all-too-human Captain James Kirk—impulsive, emotional, and driven as much by passion and hope as by anything else—and his coldly logical, emotionally immune first officer, Spock.

Of course, many of the story lines are resolved by the two characters working together—the combination of emotion, instinct, and logic—but the tension between the two is always at the heart of the story. In episode after episode, Spock's eyebrows arch at an improbable angle to underline his disapproval of Kirk and company's behavior. Even to a half-Vulcan, humans are disappointingly "illogical."

Many economists and other students of human behavior share this disappointment. Indeed, perhaps the most important general scientific finding about human behavior of the last half century is how often and how blatantly we fail to live up to the standards of rationality set both by Spock and by classical economics. Whether you consider the conformity research of psychologists such as Stanley Milgram and Philip Zimbardo, inspired by the cruelties inflicted by humans on each other, or the behavioral economics pioneered by Daniel Kahnemann and popularized by Richard Thaler and Cass Sunstein in *Nudge*, the hard truth about humans is this: we are beset with emotions and cognitive biases, and much of the time we avoid thinking altogether. We are not the calculating, rational creatures that we'd like to imagine we are.

If we were, it would be so much easier to organize things for the common good. For one thing, we could ameliorate many of the problems of the modern world—obesity, smoking, alcohol abuse, sexually transmitted diseases—simply by providing individuals with the relevant information, much as politicians and health profession-als suggest, trusting individuals to decide for themselves and behave accordingly. If only humans were that straightforward! But we're not. Actually—and happily, to our way of thinking—we're a lot more interesting than that. Our goal here is to show how the uniquely *social* nature of human evolution and behavior shapes the manner in which culture evolves among collections of individuals, particu-larly huge masses of individuals in modern societies.

PLAYBOY AND THE PLEISTOCENE

If you're still worried about being "disappointingly human," perhaps you can blame evolution—something that's often represented nar-rowly as ancient biological selection that channeled behavior into optimal packages, genetically transmitted for thousands of genera-tions without change. When Jerome Barkow, Leda Cosmides, and John Tooby published *The Adapted Mind* in 1992, evolutionary psy-chology went mainstream. The exciting idea was that our brains were hard-wired with behavioral tendencies that evolved on the savannas of Africa during the two million years of the Pleistocene, long after our hominin ancestors came down out of the trees and started wandering around on two legs. Certain behavioral regulari-ties seemed to support this notion. People on a whole prefer savan-nas to every kind of environment but the one they were raised in. Women can remember the relationship among objects on a table better than men can—seemingly a holdover from their "gather-ing" past. Men are better at holding larger-scale geographic mental maps—a holdover from their "hunting" past.

What opened the imaginations of researchers and the public alike was the suggestion that these evolved tendencies, which were adapted for a landscape full of natural dangers, a hunting-and-gathering lifestyle, and sexual games that were played out in small groups, had stuck with us and were now running up against a very different environment. This seemed to imply that we are trapped in Pleistocene bodies in the middle of modern technology and facing a totally different set of social norms. Could this be true? Apparently a lot of researchers thought so, and they tried to explain many of our modern behaviors in terms of "misplaced" Pleistocene instincts—what Sir Thomas Browne was getting at in *Religio Medici* (1643) when he proclaimed, "there is all Africa and her prodigies in us." So, for example, driving a Bentley or playing jazz became for some evolutionary psychologists a costly signaling strategy for males to attract females, much as a peacock's tail does. Similarly, acquiring a lifelong taste for a favorite food, such as Ding Dongs (Oprah) or fried peanut butter and banana sandwiches (Elvis), became a manifestation of our evolved sense of trusting wild foods that did not kill us.

Evolutionary psychology *is* all about food and sex—especially sex, with a full-blown branch of science now devoted to how our sexual attractions evolved. The early days of evolutionary sex research were rather hedonistic, exemplified by a study of *Playboy* centerfolds from the 1950s to the 1980s that suggested the presence of some strongly biologically rooted and thus immutable tendencies in what males find attractive in women's bodies. In comparing waist-to-hip ratios in centerfold models over the decades, researchers found that it was constant at about 0.7. Why? Were hips that are one-third wider than waists indicative of youth and greater fertility?

In the same study, roughly a hundred college males were shown a set of line drawings of female figures in one-piece bathing suits, in a range of different waist-to-hip ratios. The students preferred women with the same waist-to-hip ratio as in the centerfolds—0.7. Brain scans of young males taken while they looked at pictures of naked women demonstrated that this optimal waist-to-hip ratio activates neural reward centers in men—again, an "obvious" holdover from our Pleistocene life on the savanna.

The 1993 *Playboy* study has been cited hundreds of times and has led to a cascade of academic research. For example, researchers have left *Playboy* on the table and headed for exotic dance clubs, where they've discovered that lap dancers make more tips when they are ovulating and therefore giving off more sexual signals. Other researchers are happy to go out to regular nightclubs—or, shall we say, "human sexual display grounds"—where dancing women compete for male attention, especially the attention of wealthy and healthy males.

These dance-club studies are an amusing niche, and the wider research into attractiveness has found some interesting regularities as well as exceptions. Among the main findings are that both men and women prefer facial symmetry, which again is rationalized as indicating reproductive health, even though a woman's facial symmetry has not convincingly been linked empirically to the health of her baby. Another interesting result is the repeated demonstration that a woman prefers a more masculine face (more angular) when she is ovulating than she does during the rest of her monthly cycle. This is true for male voices, too. Women prefer a more masculine voice when ovulating and a higher, more "caring" male voice the rest of the time.

Although studies show clear regularities in what modern people find attractive in each other, biology is far from the only factor involved in human mating behavior. A DNA study that tracked Y-chromosome lineages in Central Asia suggested that Genghis Khan was the male ancestor of about 8 percent of all current males in a large section of Asia. This sounds difficult to believe—that a man who died around eight hundred years ago could be responsible for that large a percentage of a huge population—but we *should* believe it. Although the Mongols were polygynous, and Genghis Kahn was a particular opportunist in this respect, his long-term reproductive success was not simply a result of how many children he himself had, but also of how successful his male children were at reproducing, and their male children after them. From all appearances, they were incredibly successful—a success brought about in no small part by the fact that they were direct descendants of Genghis Khan. Khan's offspring, and their offspring, and so on down the line must have been social magnets in terms of attracting mates.

Perhaps this sheds some further light on the attractiveness studies. How fixed *are* preferences, and how much are they subject to social and cultural influences? Would female features that appealed to Genghis Khan appeal to modern Western males? Probably not. Attractiveness changes with fashion—contrast the waiflike heroine look of the late 1990s with the plumpness of the Enlightenment and Romantic eras, when well-placed body fat was an attractive display of wealth. This is still true of developing world societies in which diet is not abundant: fatness and pear-shaped figures are seen as attractive.

In a study published in 1998, Douglas Yu and Glenn Shepard took the same line drawings used in the *Playboy* centerfold study, several of which are shown below, to several indigenous communities and showed them to some of the males. In the Amazon, men preferred, not surprisingly, more pear-shaped figures (what could look healthier?). A Matsigenka man from a small community in southeastern Amazonian Peru thought that the American hourglass figure made a woman appear as if she had diarrhea, and he ranked one of the thinner figures as "pale, almost dead." Clearly, attractiveness is at least partly cultural. Not all males in remote indigenous communities like a plump figure—the hourglass shape is popular in the highlands of Papua New Guinea—and norms of attractiveness change through time and across societies. They also vary among individuals.

Thus it is worth asking how appropriate it is to appeal to our Pleistocene roots when explaining attractiveness and mate selection

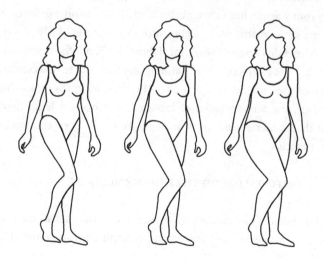

today. Modern society is characterized by hundreds, thousands, or even billions more choices than were available to the prehistoric small groups in which our hominin ancestors evolved. We see literally thousands of potential partners in the urban world or on online dating and social-networking sites, the vast majority of whom are quite healthy, well presented, and available. This is hardly prehistoric society, where mate choices were meager (even allowing for the fact that mates could be captured from neighboring groups), breath was pretty bad (you should see the cavities in the teeth of prehistoric farmers), and pathologies were common.

From the beginning of recorded history, marriage and sex were as much about social obligations as anything else. The Yanomamö of the Amazon rain forest, for example, have long practiced sister exchange, in which allied communities take turns exchanging brides from one generation to the next. A girl is often promised at a very young age to her future husband and has virtually no choice in the matter. In matrilineal societies such as the Iroquois of New York, men depended on their wives for rights to land, but the upside was that they were left free to travel around and hunt, trade, and conduct war—all the "manly" things in life. The point is, in strong kinship systems, the idiosyncrasies of love and romance are less important than wider social forces such as group alliances and wealth inheritance.

THE FOREST FOR THE TREES: THE SOCIAL SIDE OF THINGS

Explanations of evolutionary psychology often make sense, but they often seem to work only for a world of small kinship groups. Left out is humans' *social*, not just sexual, nature. We live in, and are adapted to, a social landscape of *other people*. Today, that means lots and lots of other people, far more than during the vast majority of our (always ongoing) biological evolution. Millions gather in Mecca for the annual Hajj pilgrimage, which is on the order of the population of the world 10,000 years ago. Michigan Stadium in Ann Arbor holds 110,000 football spectators, which is nearly the population of Rome in 500 B.C. There are so many people that our social brains, which anthropologist Robin Dunbar proposes evolved for living in groups of 150 or fewer, must surely be overwhelmed.

All of this shows why human societies, inhabited by social creatures, are governed by patterns that extend well beyond the individual. Love, marriage, and sex are patterned differently depending on which scale we're using. We think we understand sexual relationships at the individual level, but this gives us almost no ability to predict things at the population level. However, both levels matter when we're confronting big issues such as the spread of HIV, which is mediated by individual behaviors but manifest at the population scale by an incredible diversity of those behaviors and their interactions. Not only do we need to know whether we are whale hunters or hunter-gatherers but, as we will see throughout the book, we need to realize that there are patterns of behavior that are not even predictable from *group* norms.

What makes sense on the Pleistocene savanna or in laboratory settings with a few people often doesn't translate to such massive populations—and not just a few other people known to us but hundreds or thousands or millions of other people, depending on the context. By way of analogy, consider all that botanists know about the biology of trees and the nature of the processes that govern their growth. A great deal of this arboricultural detail is irrelevant when officials battle a forest fire or when our prehistoric ancestors used controlled burning to manage landscapes for hunting and gathering. As we will describe more in chapter 5, a good "cascade" model of forest-fire spread treats the trees simply as flammable occupants of a grid, in which a tree is lit by a burning tree in the neighboring grid square. When we move up a scale, to trees in the forest, what we know about, say, the various tissues of a tree is not what we need to explain the frequency and spread of forest fires.

We may remind ourselves not to miss the forest for the trees, but we often do it anyway. We read about the latest experiment on people choosing between chocolate bars and potato chips in a psychology lab, or about the area of the brain that lights up when a woman calculates the diameter of a circle, and we generalize it to wider society—how people will purchase products, react to a crisis, or change their daily habits of energy conservation. The generalization never quite works, though, not because the experiments are somehow wrong but because "more" really is different. This realization has shed considerable light on herd behavior, with people as "social atoms," as physicist Mark Buchanan put it. We are, however, not just social atoms. In most social situations it doesn't really help to think of us colliding into each other and traveling away with conservation of momentum and energy, or diffusing across space indiscriminately. Our forces of interaction are much different than that.

The key to fitting the pieces together is in identifying the essential social aspects of human beings at the appropriate level of complexity—not so overly simple as billiard balls or omniscient rational actors but not so overly detailed either, like the neurotic patient in Freudian psychoanalysis. It is difficult to imagine that evolution could work on each of our favorite aspects of human behavior separately and then cobble them together at the same time into a single human. Similarly, we can't think of the evolution of one technological element of an automobile, such as the fuel-injection system, without thinking of how it coevolved with other elements, such as spark-plug wires. One way to do this is to grow things in a treelike manner—the tack we took in writing this book.

ORGANIZING OUR THINKING AS TREES

This kind of embeddedness is surely a factor in the evolution of the human brain and the regularities of behavior that emerged in an intensely social way of adapting to the world. In other words, rather than a montage of different, highly specific adaptations to account for all our behaviors, perhaps there is a more minimalist architecture. All vertebrates, for example, are unified by their embeddedness within an underlying shared ancestry of skeletal development. This may apply to behavioral adaptations as well. The theory of "universal moral grammar" is the idea that an innate, deep-seated logic of morality is hard-wired into the human brain, much like the universal grammar linguist Noam Chomsky once proposed. One of the most interesting debates connected to both universal morality and universal grammar is whether they evolved as complex adaptations or as a minimal set of rules that grew out of the human brain's neural architecture, with no need for special adaptation.

This architecture allows for the recursive nature of language, which simply means we can embed bits of our sentences into one another and even embed sub-bits into those bits, and so on. The recursive nature of language is both a common feature of human languages and unique to humans. Indeed, the recursive syntax (structure) of human language may underlie its semantics (meaning). This hierarchical structure is what enables human cognition. If the recursive organization of language proceeds from the hierarchical structure of neuronal activity, it may follow that some treelike organization of information retrieval in the human brain preceded language evolution.

The human brain is unique in that it can remember those embedded bits long enough to resolve them into a sequence. Consider the sentence, "In the late 1980s, Reginald worked at the movie theatre, which cost 99 cents for all movies and where the custodian would arrive at 1:00 a.m. dressed in a tank-top and scour the seats for loose change, which was razed to make room for the Methodist church parking lot in 1996." Understanding this sentence requires two things. First, it requires a working memory of how the sequence of words has progressed, given that to the thought is finished only at the end. Second, it requires a recursive means of organizing the embedded parts of the sentence. Morality can be thought of in this way. Picture a Mafia drama where the boss of one family treats his daughter with reverence but has no qualms about roughing up the son of his father's old nemesis in a rival family. This, too, requires a working memory and a treelike thinking: up a generation to the father, over to another branch to the father's enemy, and back down to the father's enemy's son.

Here we can see a similar basic architecture between how we think about everyday sentences and how we think about the kinship relations that have conditioned the ways in which humans organize their interactions within related groups and between groups. Perhaps this treelike thinking is inherent in a number of different animal species, but only humans have the working memory to reach back up the branches and back down again to connect the leaves of a recursive relationship. In fact, working memory is one of the crucial cognitive adaptations that made humans unique from other species, as such memory is needed to make a stone hand axe, for example.

If our assertions up to this point are correct, we can see that several supposed "universal" aspects of human behavior—the deep architecture of language, the manner in which kinship relations are regarded, and possibly some generalities of our moral grammar—could be conditioned by a treelike organization of working memory. There need be no special adaptations to account for each of these behavioral regularities. The similarity comes mainly from a simple structural architecture underlying them. If so, then there is plenty of room for variation in the branches—variation in systems of morality, in ways of speaking, and in ways of regarding kinship. Of course, this is exactly what we see in the five thousand or so different languages today, to say nothing of countless past languages that have disappeared.

We also see it in the huge range in kinship systems used around the world and in cultural variation in morality. The simple facts that morals differ from one society to the next and that our own view of fairness can change over time are enough to assure us that there is no one universal rationality shared by all people at all times—or even by a significant fraction of people at a single point in time. There may be a common mental architecture from which our morals derive, but there is no specific, universal morality. Instead, we have *cultures*, where people share *social norms* for some length of time. People of a culture generally agree on them, yet no one specifically designed them. How might we account for such cooperation in groups? Let's turn the page and find out.

RULES OF THE GAME

To other musicians, drummers and their supposed stupidity are a source of perpetual amusement. For example, how do you tell if the stage is level? See if the drummer's dribbling out of both sides of his mouth. So when Pat Kane, the semiretired lead singer of Scottish pop group Hue & Cry, considered his drummer's self-proclaimed "Protestant work ethic," he wondered whether the opposite might represent our modern world just as well. In other words, is *play* a lens through which we can understand much of human behavior? Kane's book, *The Play Ethic*, is an excellent guide to this perspective on humanity.

To play is to interact. Play involves multiple individuals, which takes us beyond one-off studies of isolated individuals and their preferences for potato chips or *Playboy* centerfolds. As economist

Thomas Schelling has put it, most human life consists of individuals responding to a context of other individuals' responses to other individuals. As the name implies, game theory is a good place to start to understand that context, because it involves the kinds of repeated interactions with others that characterize modern life. Game theory provides us with insights into not only the *patterns* of social evolution but also the *processes*.

Game theory started out with simple one-on-one games and then over the years moved on to more complicated, multiplayer games. The classic prisoner's dilemma game is one of the simplest to play. Here's the question it asks: why would two people refuse to cooperate even when it is in their best interests to do so? The gist of the game is that the police arrest two suspects, but they have insufficient evidence for convictions and so try and make a deal with each suspect. If one informs on the other, he goes free and the other one gets a five-year sentence. If both stick with their alibis and neither betrays the other, they each get a six-month sentence. If they *both* turn informant, they get sentences somewhere in the middle. What should they do? The "rational"—but more like "paranoid"—outcome is for both prisoners to defect and rat on the other and thus both lose.

One of the more interesting developments in game theory came about through a computer tournament that political scientist Robert Axelrod staged in 1984, in which researchers were invited to submit their prisoner's dilemma strategies. The tournament featured strategies in which contestants played each other one-on-one for a number of rounds, called the repeated prisoner's dilemma game. The idea was to see which strategy did best in one-on-one contests against all other strategies. As opposed to the one-off game, in which all rational actors defect, the winner was the "tit-for-tat" strategy, submitted by Anatol Rapoport. The tit-for-tat strategy was dumb copying par excellence: cooperate if the other player just cooperated, defect if the other player just defected.

The strategy had a utopian aspect to it. If two contestants playing each other both used tit-for-tat, they could cooperate back and forth indefinitely, as long as the game got off on the right foot by the players cooperating first. This happy equilibrium was disrupted if one player "accidentally" defected, which would set off a cycle of cooperate–defect between the players (one defects while the other cooperates, and then vice versa, indefinitely). If another accidental defection occurred, then tit-for-tat went into the tank.

All this sounds terribly robotic. Some of us probably have no trouble seeing how games like prisoner's dilemma might be useful in helping to explain the behavior of microbes, where such simple, algorithmic rules seem quite reasonable, but we have difficulty seeing how they apply to humans, who are more capricious and variable and who certainly don't just play isolated one-on-one games with each other. A good conversation between two people conceivably could have some tit-for-tat aspects to it (trading bits of gossip, for example), but if a third person joins in, the conversation inevitably changes direction, often unpredictably. In politics, this was just the effect minority candidate Nick Clegg had on the Cameron–Brown debate in Britain in 2010 and Ross Perot had on the Bush–Clinton debate in the United States in 1992. With even more people involved, conversations often veer in random directions: "Why are we now talking about goats when we began by talking about concrete?" This kind of fun would never happen between two players simulated by game theory: "Let's eat." "You first." "No, you first." "No, *you*." "You first." "Let's eat." The point is, two-player game theory cannot possibly account for the unpredictability of interesting conversation.

It pays to start simply, however, because complexity can easily be added. Over the years, different dimensions of variability have been added incrementally to prisoner's dilemma to determine how they affect the outcomes. With respect to spatial relationships, for example, players could compete against those adjacent to them or they could meet randomly.

Perhaps what provided the most insight was to view the players not in a geographic space but rather in a network, given that people interact in social networks. Would self-interest again guide outcomes? Not really. At the Northwestern University Institute on Complex Systems, in Chicago, Luis Amaral, Brian Uzzi, and other researchers examine how team performance—in realms as diverse as sports, Broadway musicals, and scientific research—depends not only on the individuals of the team but also on how they cooperate. Concerned especially with the progress of science, now increasingly practiced by large research teams, the Northwestern group finds that individual statistics can be a poor predictor of team performance.

Indeed, much of the evolutionary success of humans as a species is due to cooperation. Feeble fodder for predators on our own, humans are formidable in cooperative groups. Harvard game theorist Martin Nowak and his team found that cooperation can evolve in a social network either through a we-versus-them group mentality, or else through some form of reciprocity. They showed how cooperation is able to evolve if and only if the benefits of cooperating outweigh the costs paid by individuals. This can happen more easily in social networks that are more tightly clustered and have fewer friends per person. More generally, Nowak has proposed five conditions for the evolution of cooperation: kin selection and group selection, and direct, indirect, and network reciprocity. We can lump these into three categories: group mentality, reciprocity, and reputation.

Group mentality can foster cooperation because we help those who are biologically related to us (kin selection) or those who are in the same group (group selection). The latter is generally the more reasonable for humans because even though there are important demonstrations of kin selection—nepotism and wealth inheritance are classic examples—we clearly cooperate with all sorts of people in such ways as market exchange or specialization within a group that allows us to, say, hunt a whale or build and defend a settlement, which benefits everyone in the group. Successful groups then can spread at the expense of other groups.

Reciprocity can foster cooperation in the direct way that tit-for-tat achieves it—I'll cooperate if you cooperate first—but *direct reciprocity* can be unstable, in that a few defectors can kill the mood. Also, direct reciprocity does not explain why people cooperate with individuals whom they have never met before and may never meet again. A more powerful theory for human society is *indirect reciprocity*. In this case, we might cooperate because cooperation is in the air—others whom we have met before have cooperated and we generally follow suit. The English don't say "please" a lot in response to some specific kindness; they just do it because it is all around them.

Reputation also enables indirect reciprocity. We can all think of examples in which having a good reputation in one sphere does not mean having a good reputation in another. The long-running HBO series *The Sopranos* created wonderful characters who simultaneously held excellent and rock-bottom reputations, depending on the social context. Anthropologists love reputation and how it gets expressed. A classic example is the potlatch feast held by a Northwest Coast chief, whose aim is to give away as much food as possible in order to boost his own status. The same occurs in central Mexico, where individual males or even entire households carry out religious and secular duties for a year, including paying for fiestas and other celebrations. It might come close to bankrupting them, but you'll never hear them complain. They're too busy enjoying the increased status their largesse produces.

Reputation, of course, works only if people recognize you and what you are reputed for. Similarly, group membership and kinship require some form of identification tag (what Richard Dawkins calls the "green beard"), or we wouldn't be able to keep membership or kinship straight. In traditional societies there are clan names, lineage names, and surnames that help people keep track of which group(s) they belong to (not to mention such things as totem poles), but there are also fascinating arrays of different systems of first names that clue people in as to how to behave toward one another. Among the !Kung San of the Kalahari Desert in western Africa, names designate whether two people have a joking relationship or an avoidance relationship. This is helpful for such mobile people who may encounter distant relatives in the bush, where if it were not for the naming system they might not know each other well enough to know what is proper behavior and what is not.

There are countless other tags that people willingly adopt to identify with one group or another—accents, "virgin" rings among Christian youth in the United States, tattoos, and so-called code words used by the political media to grab the attention of the Left or the Right. People also tag themselves through appearance. Bankers, snowboarders, goateed computer programmers, football fans in England, and soccer moms in the United States—each has a fairly standard outfit, hairstyle, and favorite mode of transportation. You can buy eyeglasses to make you look "quirky." Other glasses say "six-figure salary." Some say "architect schooled in French philosophy" or "might explode at any moment."

The key to group membership, of course, is copying those around you so that when you're in Rome you act as the Romans do, and not like someone else. We know from our daily lives that group inclusion is often more important than individuality, and sometimes it even defines fairness (consider the different forms of taxation around the world) or what is rational. We see this in non-Western cultures as well. In a series of field experiments coordinated by anthropologist Joe Henrich, laboratory games normally played with Western university students were played instead in over a dozen different traditional societies from around the world, each making a living in a different way and involving different degrees of cooperation and market integration. The Lamelera whale hunters of Indonesia, for example, rely on intensive cooperation during the hunt, where every male has his role on the boat and the whale that is killed will feed the entire community. The Hadza hunter-gatherers of Tanzania, by contrast, forage as nomadic, often nuclear family groups. In some societies there exist markets for the exchange of goods, which is quite different from individual barter or competitive feasting, where the object is to give away as much food as possible.

In each setting, researchers put the equivalent of $100 on the table between two people and asked one of them to give as much as he or she liked to the other. In Western societies, among American university students, for example, the average amount usually given away is $50, considered "fair" by both parties, and any offer that is "unfairly" low—say, below $20—will be contemptuously rejected. Even though this violates the economic ideal of rationality, according to which givers should keep all and receivers should be happy to receive anything, Westerners see 50 percent as normal—so normal, in fact, that it is often assumed to be a human universal.

Fifty percent, however, is not universal at all. In the cross-cultural experiment, different societies made quite different average offers. Among the Lamelera whale hunters, the typical offer was significantly greater than 50 percent of the pot, and in some instances close to 90 percent. Among the Hadza, however, the average offer was less than 35 percent. Among the Machiguenga horticulturalists of southeastern Peru, the average offer was even lower, 26 percent, and only a tenth of offers below 20 percent were rejected. Further, these were not scattered results. Rather, each society tended to have a well-defined average offer, normally distributed around a clear average value. In other words, each society had a well-defined, distinct cultural norm of fairness.

These concepts are understandable from an evolutionary standpoint when we consider the ways in which these cultures make a living. Among the intensely cooperative Lamelera, average offers were very high because the concept of sharing was derived from the whale hunt, which feeds everyone. In contrast, groups that were normally much more self-reliant, such as the Machiguenga, who practice slash-and-burn horticulture in independent family units, were much less generous in their giving and also more likely to accept the sort of low offer that would be rejected by Westerners.

"Of course," we say when looking at this remarkable study. It makes perfect sense that people who survive through cooperative whaling would have a more communal, generous norm of fairness than would an individualist society, where it's everyone for him- or herself. Similarly in modern geopolitics, norms of fairness, such as might pertain to intellectual copyright, differ greatly between, say, the United States and China. The idea of fairness is relative, even within Western society, depending on the context. If you win the lottery or score big at blackjack, no one except perhaps close family would expect you to share the money with them. Yet if you *earn* your money through your own hard work, *everyone* expects you to give a fair amount of it away through income taxes. This makes no *rational* sense, but it makes perfect *cultural* sense.

Sometimes it's tough being a social animal, what with all the decisions we have to make in light of the customs and rules of our particular society. In turn, our decisions affect the group as well: we make very few decisions that don't have downstream effects. It might seem better if we were primarily solitary animals, maybe getting together for sex and a meal or two, then returning to our house in the woods for months at a time. Few solitary individuals exist, however, because survival requires us to know what other people in our world are doing. Fortunately we do this naturally, through our individual social brains and our collective social minds—the topics of the next chapter.

3

COPYING BRAIN, SOCIAL MIND

Psychologist Nicholas Humphrey spent considerable time early in his career in Africa, first with Dian Fossey, studying gorillas, and then with Richard Leakey, studying the remains of our hominin ancestors. This experience fundamentally changed his views on what the brains of the great apes, us included, are for. In his essay "The Social Function of Intellect," Humphrey describes his view:

During two months I spent watching gorillas in the Virunga mountains I could not help being struck by the fact that of all the animals in the forest the gorillas seemed to lead much the simplest existence—food abundant and easy to harvest (provided they knew where to find it), few if any predators (provided they knew how to avoid them) . . . little to do in fact (and little done) but eat, sleep and play.

Humphrey acknowledged that the kinds of cognitive feats and abilities demonstrated by human and nonhuman apes in the laboratory were rare in the field. They just didn't seem to be part of day-to-day life:

I have yet to hear of any example from the field of a chimpanzee (or for that matter a Bushman) using his full capacity for inferential reasoning in the solution of a biologically relevant practical problem. Someone may retort that if an ethologist had kept watch on Einstein through a pair of field glasses he might well have come to the conclusion that Einstein too had a hum-drum mind. But that is just the point: Einstein, like the chimpanzees, displayed his genius at rare times in "artificial" situations— he did not use it, for he did not need to use it, in the common world of practical affairs.

Humphrey saw that the brains of higher primates are complex organs built in large part for *social* functions. Primates aren't the only social animals, but they do it at levels unseen in other animals. Primate brains can solve economic problems—all animal brains do this—but primate brains allow their holders to solve *social* problems and to do it at an advanced level. As a result, even chimpanzee groups develop distinct behavioral cultures, as Andrew Whiten, Jane Goodall, and many other primatologists found when comparing their field observations from chimpanzee populations across Africa.

The human brain is the most social of all primate brains by orders of magnitude. It doesn't *dictate* what we do socially; its importance lies in what it *allows* us to do and to do rapidly. Social interactions require the ability to represent mentally the beliefs of others (whether similar or different), which we do automatically, even as infants. The best way to view this is by comparing ourselves to our ancestors of 40,000 years ago, the beginning of what archaeologists commonly refer to as the Upper Paleolithic period, or the Late Stone Age.

MORE REALLY *IS* DIFFERENT

With a few exceptions, we are not any different biologically than we were back then. Yes, after millennia of agriculture some populations are now lactose tolerant, and those of us with a West African ancestry are more susceptible to a distortion of red blood cells than those of us with a European ancestry, but these are not anything that would separate us as a species from our ancestors sixteen hundred generations ago. If there were any reason to place us in a separate box it would be strictly on social grounds, not on anything biological. The key to the box is the level of interconnectedness that we have with one another.

There is more to this statement than just our living in larger groups than our ancestors did or having different social obligations. It refers to a much more profound reality, that what goes through our minds is derived in no small part from what goes through the minds of those around us. As a result, what we are thinking is just an extension, or a sample, of what is being thought around us. The more people around us, the more potential storage area there is, not to mention the greater the chance for innovation to occur. What happens when we live in a society with just sixty people as opposed to several thousand? Not only do we have less knowledge collectively, we also have less knowledge individually and undoubtedly a simpler frame of reference.

Take, for example, the Pirahã, a small, remote group of hunter-gatherers living in villages along the Maici River in northwestern Brazil. Their language lacks cardinal and ordinal numbers, and they apparently experience only the present, such that when someone leaves a village, those remaining *literally* think the person has left the universe. The Pirahã language is interesting from another, controversial, standpoint. Linguist Daniel Everett claims that Pirahã lacks recursion—the phenomenon we mentioned in chapter 1 whereby phrases or sentences can be embedded in other phrases or sentences into infinity. Noam Chomsky and others would argue that Pirahã does *not* lack recursion because it is the universal feature that makes human language unique. Regardless, Pirahã is not only different in major ways from other languages, it is structurally "simpler" than most other languages. It also is much simpler today than it was several hundred years ago, when the Pirahã split from the larger native population of the Mura.

It is possible that the Pirahã lost much of their knowledge in the population bottleneck that resulted. This would be similar to you and some friends trying to pass on the knowledge of your entire society to your kids. It's impossible to do. The Pirahã lost so much, perhaps, that not only did their language become simpler, so too did their very thoughts. This wouldn't make their thoughts inferior—obviously, they serve the Pirahã well—just less complex. How do we define complex in this situation? Maybe we start with a definition that takes into account the amount of knowledge that can be stored collectively and retrieved effectively. Not surprising, the amount is determined in large part by group size.

Obviously, there is no one-to-one correlation between group size and amount of storage such that if we know one, we can determine the other. The social environment partly determines how and when people learn, as does our biological background. A twelve-year-old learns differently than an adult does, although the differences have more to do with rate of learning than with the processes of learning. Although biological evolution always continues, the human brain of today, in terms of wiring and the like, is not substantially different from that of 40,000 years ago. What is different is the intensity of social interaction and the cognitive demands of interaction, which get ratcheted up within increasingly larger social groups.

WHY COPY?

Anthropologist Robin Dunbar's social-brain hypothesis is analogous to Nicholas Humphrey's primate-brain hypothesis. Dunbar maintains that the human brain, energetically expensive compared to that of nonhuman primates, has social relations as its evolutionary raison d'être, especially for all the complexities of sexual relations. As we pointed out in chapter 1, our brains are not the rational computers that classical economics presupposes. Rather, as behavioral economics suggests, our brains use shortcuts and heuristics to monitor the brains around them.

Among the most intriguing physical mechanisms we have for this are mirror neurons in the brain. Mirror neurons were discovered by accident when a researcher, on the team led by Italian neuroscientist Giacomo Rizzolatti in 1992, moved a nut and measured how the brain of a macaque monkey fired in a way similar to when the monkey itself moved the nut. The neurons help the monkey's brain mirror what's going on in other monkeys' brains around it. Marco Iacoboni and colleagues subsequently identified many more, subtly differentiated types in the human brain's premotor and inferior parietal cortexes. Our brains are rich with mirror neurons. They compel us to intuit quickly each other's intentions and even to empathize. Mirror neurons imply we are social creatures at the deepest level. As Iacoboni told Gordy Slack, "The self and the other are just two sides of the same coin. To understand myself, I must recognize myself in other people."

So we are wired to copy, but what is the advantage of this kind of supremely social brain? Other animal species are able to learn, and a good number of them on occasion practice social learning, but humans are more accurate social imitators than any other animal yet tested. Other animals don't come close to our speed of learning by imitation, retaining what is learned, and pulling information together from widely separated locales within the brain.

Imitating others can be a highly adaptive strategy: why reinvent what someone else has already done for you? As British economist John Maynard Keynes put it in a 1937 article on employment, "Knowing that our own individual judgement is worthless, we . . . endeavour to conform with the behaviour of the majority or the average. The psychology of a society of individuals each of whom is endeavouring to copy the others leads to what we may strictly term a *conventional* judgement." Academics call this copying *social learning*, which is so central to primate behavior that there is an ever-growing literature on all the strategies that animals, including people, use to choose what or whom to copy. Some of the more well-studied strategies are

- Copy the majority
- Copy successful individuals
- Copy if better
- Copy good social learners
- Copy kin
- Copy friends
- Copy older individuals

We just employed several of those strategies when we lifted that list from an article written by our colleague Kevin Laland, an animal behaviorist at the University of St Andrews, who himself had copied the list and added to it.

In the list above, some of the copying strategies refer to skill level as the main criterion (copy those who are better at something than we are, copy good social learners, copy those who are successful), whereas others refer to social criteria (copy the majority, copy kin or friends, copy older individuals). For cultural evolution, there is a crucial difference in the effects of copying based on *selection* for the knowledge or a skill level as opposed to copying based on simple *social interaction*—the highly effective "do as the Romans do" strategy we mentioned earlier. Copying can be quite randomly directed, which leads to highly volatile collective behavior rather than to steady homogeneity. As important as this point is, it often goes unrecognized.

THE SOCIAL BRAIN: ORGANIZED IN TREES

Another benefit of a social brain is the ability to keep track of eligible and noneligible mates, which is a much more complex challenge for humans than it is for other primates. Keeping track of mates is a moving target. In any human society there is a flux of people—those being born, those dying, those marrying out, those marrying in. In kinship, genetic distance is a key organizing principle, and one of the most efficient means of keeping tabs on genetic distances is by creating a tree. We discussed this treelike thinking in chapter 1. Although we do a lot of organizing this way, from the tree of life that botanist Carl Linnaeus devised in the eighteenth century to the tree of files on most computer operating systems, it does not have to be conscious or planned. Treelike structures emerge from the simplest of growth rules, organizing themselves everywhere in nature, as in a river drainage, a real tree (obviously), or even in human vascular networks and neural networks. Similar trees also represent the hierarchical group organization of social mammals such as baboons and orca whales.

Social primates such as baboons organize themselves through hierarchical classification derived from individual rank and kinship, but because humans are unlikely to know all members of their community, the organization is sustained by overlapping networks of kinship, marriage, and friendship. At the scale of individuals, the division of labor between men (hunting) and women (gathering) is reinforced through pair bonding, partly through food sharing, to reduce risk. At a larger scale, the band or tribe serves as a social unit that often resolves tensions between dispersion and

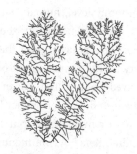

River system

Kinship

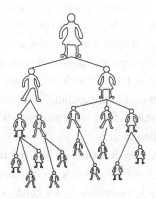

Organization

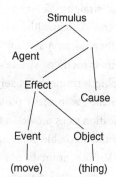

Thought

interdependence. At the wider community level, humans sustain social relations through gift exchange, marriage, fiestas, and the like.

Maintaining such systems is made much easier with the use of names or some other classificatory device. Names might be the easiest if only a few people are involved—Bob, Olivia, Logan, and so on—but with more people, we want to devise terms that lump certain people together—"uncle," for example—and split them out from others—"aunts" and "grandmothers." As we mentioned in chapter 2, some groups, such as the !Kung San of the Kalahari Desert, structure their behavior according to kinship, maintaining joking relations with certain kin (as indicated by their name) and serious avoidance relations with others. To keep their mating potential straight, Yanomamö males of the Amazon refer to their female cross cousins (the daughters of their mothers' brothers and their fathers' sisters) as "wife" and their parallel cousins (the daughters of their mothers' sisters and their fathers' brothers) as "sister." As kinship terminologies serve a number of functions, they must be adaptable, with many possible states of the terminology system. Classification trees provide a flexible solution.

By some debatable point in prehistory, humans had full language ability. Various animals can communicate through grunts, alarm calls, or even sign language, but only humans—even a child—can construct a variety of sentences that is literally unlimited in possibility. Humans had this ability no later than 40,000 years ago, by which point biologically modern humans had spread across Europe at the expense of dwindling Neanderthal populations. The potent combination of language, group cooperation, and brainpower allowed modern humans to organize and store information with unprecedented sophistication, not only for hunting and gathering but also for social relations and mating competition. Humans have the ability to store and organize a great deal of information about their social relations, which can get complicated fast—a few siblings, dozens of cousins, scores of less-related kin, different rules for mother's side versus father's side, and so on. Kinship is central to human reproduction, and to organize it, many human cultures use simplified classification schemes, which get remembered and reinforced through daily social customs.

Coincident with the appearance of biologically modern humans in Europe was a sudden proliferation of cave art (at Lascaux and Chauvet in France, for example), personal adornment (jewelry and probably tattooing), and ritual (burials in which objects were placed alongside the dead, who often were covered with powdered iron ore). Archaeologists refer to this as the Upper Paleolithic Revolution. Some researchers argue that this transition represents the final stage in the evolution of the modern human mind, whereas others maintain that there were bits of art much earlier in Africa and that the modern mind evolved long before. We fall into the latter camp. But why was there such an explosion in creative expression as opposed to a slow, steady buildup?

THE SOCIAL MIND AND COLLECTIVE MEMORY

The answer may not be what was in peoples' heads but how those heads were connected. The Upper Paleolithic witnessed a population surge in Europe: more people were around to have new ideas and to pass on those ideas to other people before they died. This is why models of prehistory must consider population size, as exemplified by the work of our colleagues Adam Powell, Stephen Shennan, and Mark Thomas. They showed we do not necessarily need biological changes in individual cognition to explain the explosion of cultural evolution seen in Europe during the Upper Paleolithic. All we need is a fairly large, interconnected population. Population size is important, but the key point is that people are interconnected.

Rock art dominated the Upper Paleolithic, but sometime during the fourth millennium B.C. writing appeared in China, Mesopotamia, the Indus Valley, and Egypt. It was first used mainly as a form of bookkeeping, then was extended to more expressive forms. Even at that point writing was limited to a few individuals, such as the scribes of Egypt and the keepers of the code of Hammurabi in Babylon, but as writing became more creative and more expressive, from the Greek writers of tragedy to Chaucer, Shakespeare, and finally the novelists of the eighteenth century, writing became a means for the few to communicate to the many, either through performance or, later, through readings by members of literary societies. Mass broadcast media are just the logical extreme of this trend.

Overall, human prehistory and history show us that the larger a group becomes, the more information gets stored in the collected minds of its individuals. This "wisdom of crowds," an old notion that James Surowiecki popularized in his book of the same name, is why the independent guesses of many people on the weight of a cow at the county fair average so close to the correct weight, or why the Iowa opinion markets have done better at predicting national elections than the Gallup Poll. As Princeton biologist Iain Couzin put it, even simple forms of animal social learning give the group "higher-order computational capacities" to respond to its environment. A group of animals migrates long distances through lots of "noisy" directional cues that are smoothed out and integrated across the group, through social learning between individuals. Psychology experiments at Carnegie Mellon University now show how a group of people with average intelligence can brainstorm better and plan their shopping better that smarter individuals.

In the Internet age, it has become easier to see ourselves as storing information outside our own minds—on websites and in computers, for example—but we can't forget that we also store information in other people, in essence creating a social Wikipedia. When we ask someone about something, we are retrieving information stored in that person. You might, for example, store most of your knowledge about Freud in your friend Pat's mind. If you need to know something, you could just ask Pat, "Hey—what did Freud say about archaeology?" Similarly, you might store in another friend your knowledge about the first twenty pages of Proust's *Remembrance of Things Past*, which is all he's read of the seven volumes.

Sharing specialized knowledge is so commonplace, we often don't think about it. All good managers, whether at Katz's Deli, in a Washington committee, or on a fishing boat, understand that different people usefully serve different functions. Evolutionary anthropologist Daniel Nettle argues that wide variation in human personality—an evolutionary puzzle—is adaptive in itself. Thinking back to our discussion of Genghis Khan in chapter 1, we see that he was highly successful in spreading his genes, but would any parents want *all* their children to act like Kahn? It is probably better to have more cooperative siblings who can, at times, either support or control the type-A personality in the group. Humans seem to be comfortable with different roles, especially in families, and novels such as *Brothers Karamazov* underscore this.

These commonplace examples of specialized knowledge are the legacy of a much more crucial evolutionary development of us as social creatures. It's one thing to know what Freud might have said about archaeology (we doubt he said anything, but that's why we depend on our friend Pat), but it's quite another to have knowledge that might mean we eat tonight as opposed to going hungry. Hunter-gatherers are arguably the most generalized in terms of their knowledge because each family unit must be largely self-reliant. With the advent of agriculture in various regions of the world between 11,000 and 9,000 years ago, and the beginnings of villages and eventually towns and cities, accumulated knowledge and skill became even more highly specialized, with some people knowing how to cultivate crops, others how to herd livestock, others how to make pottery, and so on.

During our social evolution, the more that information became segmented among specialists, the more time could be spent experimenting and refining technological "recipes." This provided a selective advantage only so long as the segmented knowledge could be collated and protected through the generations of groups engaged in collective harvesting and hunting, food sharing, group defense, and communal parenting. Our collective ability to accumulate and pass on these specialized recipes is perhaps the best evidence that human cultural evolution is primarily social. Without the ability to store specialized information in each other, there would be no language and, we presume, no civilization. Through a positive feedback, presumably between specialization and accumulation, global knowledge has intensified exponentially such that the amount of specialized knowledge in the world is perhaps a billion times (give or take an order of magnitude) the technological variation of a prehistoric hunter-gatherer community.

Certainly a lot of modern specialized knowledge is neither technical nor subsistence related. Increasingly, it is largely social, from management, to celebrity, to entertainment, and so on. In 10,000 years, how did we get from there to here—from specialization of economic information to specialization of leisure information? There may be a fairly well-researched history of events that led from point A to point Z, but there certainly is no generally agreed-on process for the continual diversification of cultural niches and, consequently, the steady, geometric increase in skill and knowledge that characterizes human evolution.

One thing is clear: with this incredible proliferation of variation came even more chances for evolution to strike, often in surprising ways. As with biological evolution, cultural evolution needs three and only three things for it to work. It needs a source of variation— mutations in biology, inventions in culture; it needs a means of transmitting the variants—genetics in biology, learning in culture; and it needs the means to sort the variants into what we'll call "winners" and "losers"—selection (both natural and cultural) and drift.

We won't spend a lot of time looking for the source of variation; just consider the human mind with all its rich adaptations for a social world as the default generator. More interesting is how the variants diffuse across the landscape and what happens to them once they're there. We've made the case that humans are excellent copiers. Let's turn the page and find out just how good they are.

4

SOCIAL LEARNING, EN MASSE

Until the year 2000, nearly all the several thousand inhabitants of Samsø, a small island off the Danish coast, heated their houses with oil, used imported electricity, and thought little about it. Within several years, however, after organizing energy cooperatives and seminars, they had cut their fossil fuel use in half through wind power, and by 2005 the island was producing more energy from renewable sources than it was using. The turbines cost a million dollars each, so they were purchased collectively, with shareholders receiving dividend checks from the generated electricity. It was the perfect story: people made money in the long run, felt a sense of communal responsibility, and were excited just to be a part of things.

The funny thing was, these were ordinary Danish people who were not previously passionate environmentalists but who became increasingly interested and proud of their ability to become self-sufficient. Although it started with Samsø winning a government-supported contest to become Denmark's "renewable-energy island," there was otherwise no prize money, no tax breaks, not even government assistance. There was just enough funding to hire a few people to work on the project, the first of whom was Søren Hermansen, a lifelong Samsø resident.

"There was this conservative hesitating, waiting for the neighbor to do the move," Hermansen told *New Yorker* writer Elizabeth Kolbert. He repeatedly stood up at local community meetings and made his pitch for the project. Lubricating his meetings with free beer, he got his neighbors to imagine working collectively on a project in which they might all take pride. "This is where the hard work starts, convincing the first movers to be active," Hermansen said. Eventually the social dynamic began to work in favor of the project. As more people got involved, this prompted others to join in. After a while, enough islanders were participating that it became the norm. Or, as islander Ingvar Jørgensen put it, participation became a kind of sport.

Clearly, the behavior spread for social reasons and became a social norm, but this doesn't tell us *why* it spread. Every lobbyist or advertiser wants to create a new social norm these days. What made wind power on Samsø different? There were several key elements:

1. *People's direct experience was changed by the contest.*

A general contest introduces an incentive to everyone, which changes their lives directly. This contrasts with a vested interest that promotes a particular brand of behavior to the exclusion of all others, as companies do with their products. As the contest proceeded, people's direct experience was modified further.

2. *Many sparks were lit in hope of starting a fire.*

The contest itself was open to the entire country. Then, when Samsø won, the project was open to any employable volunteers. When Hermansen became the project leader, he promoted it at every opportunity, from local town meetings to everyday conversations.

3. *The community was small and socially cohesive.*

New social norms need a critical number of people, which allows a norm to overcome inertia. Also, as Malcolm Gladwell argues, norms need regular face-to-face interactions, not just online communication. In both aspects, a small community has an advantage over a larger one, at least in the beginning.

4. *The behavior had a rationale.*

Although it spread through social learning, the shift to renewable energy was economically beneficial in the long run. Further, it was gratifying as a constructive project, and it gave people something exciting to do together.

5. *The results were permanently visible and sustainable.*

By becoming part of the constructed environment, newly erected wind turbines became a highly visible source of learning for everyone.

MODELS OF SOCIAL DIFFUSION

The Samsø example shows us the change was jumpstarted by a small amount of individual learning by a few people, followed by copying by everyone else. These two elements, individual learning and copying, or social learning, are the basic ingredients of behavioral diffusion, a fundamental phenomenon of human society that has even been demonstrated to some degree among chimpanzees. Classic behavioral diffusion models are used in marketing and economics. The models work well for the rise of innovations whose benefits are obvious, such as the bow and arrow or the automobile, or even more modern behaviors such recycling, drinking bottled rather than tap water, or perhaps even taking yoga classes. The new behavior may be an intrinsically attractive option, but the knowledge of, aspiration for, or acceptance of the behavior needs to spread *socially*.

Models of social diffusion have always focused on the pattern and on very simple assumptions about how decisions are made. The main principle of these models is parsimony—seeking the fewest assumptions needed to explain the data pattern. By this philosophy, behavioral diffusion models assume that people will, on average, adopt a new idea either individually or through the influence of their peers. Although each person is different, the models assume that when you look at a population as a whole, it can be described by two probability parameters, which we can call μ and q.

The first parameter, μ, represents individual learning—the chance that at any given time a person will decide to do something on his or her own. This inspiration could be out of the blue, but it also could be prompted by information that is widely disseminated through the media. Individual learning is really any way of adopting a new behavior *except* by copying someone else, although there is one important caveat: our use of "copying" does not include learning across the generations, such as children learning from their parents or apprentices learning from masters. This, for cultural evolutionists such as Robert Boyd and Peter Richerson, is most usefully categorized as "individual learning," just over a long period of time—a "vertical" line of inherited knowledge through the generations. Guided in turn by each generation's elder mentors, knowledge can accumulate as each individual's experience is added to what gets passed down the ancestral line.

Until recently, most marketing and political conversations were mainly about individual learning, μ: make information widely available, and people will consider it on their own. More recently, however, marketers and political campaigners have become interested in the other parameter, q, which represents social learning—that is, the probability that someone will adopt a new behavior by imitation. In this classic model, a non-adopter's chance of imitation increases smoothly with the popularity of the behavior (more adopters around to copy), whereas the chance of deciding individually is always the same.

The beauty of this classic model is that it is simultaneously simple yet rich and powerful. The two parameter values, μ and q, are enough to predict a number of characteristic patterns in the adoption and subsequent abandonment of ideas within a population. Some different possibilities are shown below. In general, if the individual-learning parameter (μ) is high, then the behavior rockets up in popularity and then tails off in an exponential decay, as shown on the left. If, on the other hand, the imitation parameter (q) is dominant, then the rise and fall of the popularity curve tend to be smoother and more symmetrical, as shown on the right. In many cases, there will be a combination of both, as shown in the middle:

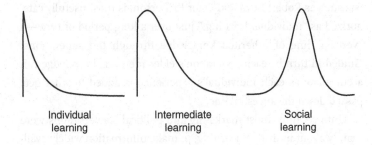

Individual learning   Intermediate learning   Social learning

These simple curves describe an astonishing range of patterns in the real world, from the spread of a new technology to that of a social norm or an idea. This does not mean we expect the curves to explain everything—far from it—but looking at these broad categories of change at the population level can help us quickly generate specific, useful hypotheses for studying a behavior more closely through interviews, ethnographic fieldwork, and so on.

It is important to note that in discussing the curves, we are talking about the rates of adoption, not the cumulative (running total) number of people who have adopted something. If we were to show the latter, then the rise and fall in the social learning (copying) case would take the form of the classic S curve. This distinction between the two measures, adoption rate and cumulative popularity, can be critical, depending on what we're looking at. If we are looking at, say, the number of people who search for a topic online each day, then we want to use the adoption rate, but if we want the total number of people who have read a particular web page after searching for it, then we want to use the cumulative figure.

Usually, one measure is clearly the more sensible. For example, people subscribe to an online club only once, so there is a limit to the cumulative number of subscribers over the short term (long term, there may be new generations of subscribers). The total number of subscribers may increase in an S curve, whereas the subscription rate may go up, peak, and then decline as all the people who were bound to subscribe have already done so. However, those subscribers, as a fixed number of people, might then look at the website at regular intervals for new content, and so the traffic on the site can go up and down from day to day. Because they can look multiple times per day, the only limit to the viewing rate might be how often the content is refreshed.

Similarly, an S curve might describe the adoption of iPhones over the medium term, given that people generally buy only one, but not the purchase of hamburgers, because one person might have a hamburger (or two) every day. You just have to think about which is the more appropriate measure for the problem—cumulative adoption or adoption rate—before applying the model.

As a point of contrast, the smoothness of the classic model highlights a fascinating possible threshold effect in online media. A study by Jukka-Pekka Onnela and Felix Reed-Tsochas of how applications are installed onto Facebook pages suggests that individual discovery of these applications dominates when they are rare, but if or when their popularity rises above a certain threshold, social learning appears to kick in abruptly. This strange jump from individual learning to social learning would not happen under the classic μ-and-q model, which is also not equipped for huge numbers of simultaneous options, as we discuss in chapter 6. The crucial tipping point is reported to be fifty-five new installations a day. Could this be when search engines or popularity lists pick them up? We don't know, but we can be certain that these kinds of studies will soon be everywhere, spreading through the academic research community, where, as we'll soon see, social learning thrives.

ANYONE FOR "LESS NUANCED"?

A good example of the adoption process that we have all experienced is the comings and goings of buzzwords. In the old days, certain slang words used to define a generation—such as "tight" to describe being drunk, as Ernest Hemmingway used it—but nowadays buzzwords and phrases often come and go in a few years, such as "under the bus," or in online or text-based communication: "LMAO!" "OMG!" Buzzwords are being picked up and adopted, passed on, and dropped for something more novel all the time, every day. One of us recently heard on the streets of Brooklyn a young girl say to her girlfriend, "knowledge is power." We doubt either was aware of the origins of that phrase in the sixteenth-century writings of Francis Bacon—"Scientia potentia est"—who himself may have borrowed it from the Book of Proverbs.

It might surprise you to think of academic jargon spreading in this way, but the same patterns are clear: each scholarly article uses words and references that have appeared in previous articles and books. That's a lot of copying, given that there are tens of thousands of academic journals, conference proceedings, edited volumes, and other academic publications on every conceivable subject, from the journal *Argumentation* (presumably about arguing), to *Wear* (a journal about friction), to *Zeolites* (the international journal of molecular sieves).

Such a mass of verbiage means that academicians are awash in titles and keywords, and like everyone else, they prefer to think of themselves as self-determining people, able to study exactly what interests them. Yet the constant flux of buzzwords and study interests suggests the tides of fashion are at play. Words such as *hysteria*, *Marxist*, and *a propos* are no longer in vogue. In their place we have words such as *nuanced*, *evidence-based*, *resilience*, and *robust*, which currently are accelerating in academic popularity. The rise of *evidence-based* and *robust*, for example, fits the copying model, as shown below.

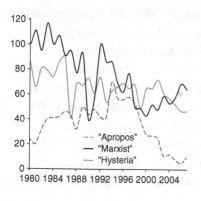
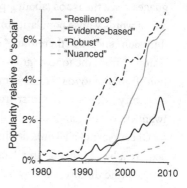

The context of a word is often copied along with it. George Orwell described this phenomenon in *Horizon* magazine back in 1946: "Modern writing at its worst does not consist in picking out words for the sake of their meaning and inventing images in order to make the meaning clearer. It consists in gumming together long strips of words which have already been set into order by someone else, and making the results printable by sheer humbug." Orwell effectively was arguing in favor of words chosen independently over strips of words copied from other people.

Orwell would not be surprised to see that, of 1,291 social science articles published between 1970 and 2010 that contained the word *nuanced*, all contained the phrase "more nuanced," but only four contained the phrase "less nuanced." Two hundred of these articles—more than 15 percent—contained the phrase "a more nuanced understanding of."

You can also compare "more nuanced" versus "less nuanced" on Google's "Ngram" viewer (ngrams.googlelabs.com), which at present scans through over five million books published in seven languages since the 1500s (about 4 percent of all books). Ngram reveals lots of words whose popularity rose and fell smoothly through social diffusion, such as "theretofore" from the late nineteenth century, "flapper" from the 1920s, "groovy" from the 1960s, and "deconstruction" from the 1970s. The rise and fall of "theretofore" took most of a century, whereas "feminist" rose in the final two decades of the twentieth century and was already on its way down by 2000.

Of course, not all words decline in this fashionable pattern if they acquire a basic function in a language, such as useful technologies or scientific discoveries ("nylon" and "virus") or figures of lasting impact (FDR, Carnegie, and Einstein). Certain popular technologies ("radio," "trombone," and "vitamin") show the social curve during the initial, "gee-whiz" stage, then settle into a more stable pattern during the later, functional stage.

It is too bad one cannot invest in academic buzzwords as we do in stocks or real estate, because buying into "nuanced" might yield a great return. Such words do have financial implications, however, because academic grants that use the right combination of buzz-words have a better chance of getting funding. In fact, an entire academic institute recently changed its name to replace the word *research* in its title to *resilience*, thereby keeping up with the buzz without having to change the "R" in the acronym. This is not only clever, it is among the most effective social learning strategies we discussed earlier: copying the successful.

WHY "COLD FUSION" IS DIFFERENT

Are there words that instead of having the social-learning pattern have the distinctive individual-learning pattern? This is uncommon, and Google's Ngram viewer shows how words for health scares (worldwide flu events), new technologies, famous brand names (Chevrolet, IBM, Coke, and Kleenex), and artists (Mozart) have followed the fairly symmetrical, social-diffusion curves. Words describing historical events ("Tiananmen," for example), however, rise very quickly and then decline in the concave-up shape of individual learning.

In academia, one good example is the phrase "cold fusion," which suddenly appeared on the academic stage after the notorious "discovery" of this theoretical energy source by Martin Fleischmann and Stanley Pons of the University of Utah in 1989. Because cold fusion, or, as it is quietly referred to today, "low-energy nuclear reaction," would have been a world-changing technology, providing vast amounts of cheap energy, many scientists took note of this well-publicized "finding" independently. As a result, we see a nice pattern of individual learning—a sharp jump on the left, followed by an exponential decline.

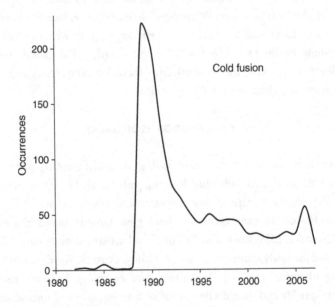

The cold fusion example reminds us of mass responses to information that do not necessarily need to spread socially. If the government announces a new tax break, or a store announces an 80

percent off sale, or the evening news covers some remarkable event, then many people will respond individually without needing to wait for anyone else. An example was the rapid decrease in driving activity following the abrupt rise in gas prices in 2008. People simply made the decision on their own to drive less because gas suddenly cost more.

Direct experience and personal relevance are powerful forces that work independent of social influence. By 1995, about 90 percent of Ugandans knew someone with AIDS, compared to 70 percent or fewer in other African countries. Equally, much of Hollywood's support for gay- and HIV-related charities stems from the direct experience of those who work in the film industry. In many cases, individual choice is the solution that well-meaning governments or health agencies may seek to promote rational independent thought. In voting, for example, we want people to make their choice independently of their peers. This is why we place such a high premium on the secrecy of the ballot box and, in some countries, why opinion polls are outlawed in at least the final days of election campaigns. Individual choice is often what we try to encourage in other areas of our lives, such as personal health, politics, and consumer purchases.

It's worth remembering that the magical wisdom of the crowd discussed in chapter 3 requires that everyone be thinking independently, so that their averaged diversity of thought yields an overall "wisdom." If they are not thinking independently, then merely supplying information, even universally, does not necessarily enhance the wisdom of crowds. Flocks gain their "wisdom" through averaging the individual perceptions of each bird, but, as Iain Couzin and colleagues point out, false alarms can spread and amplify across the flock through bad information. The element of individual thinking is crucial. When people copy others rather than thinking for themselves, their herd behavior can go wildly astray.

Social learning is why merely providing smokers, drinkers, and the obese with information about how their behavior affects their health, life expectancy, and family is unlikely to change their habits over the long term. If we want populations to *sustain* new healthy behaviors as a lifestyle change, disseminating facts and expecting people to act accordingly is insufficient.

For this reason, even though critical, informed thought might arguably be the best behavior in any population, social-influence approaches to health issues have become more widely used. Social influence is a double-edged sword, however, because it both prevents change initially and accelerates it once it gets going. We all want to know how to get our wildfires to spread. As in the Samsø case, the behavior may be taken over the tipping point through a sustained focus on a small nucleated community; this is part of the philosophy behind the U.N. Millennium Village Project, for example.

The social norm against smoking is now built not only into Western culture but also into our environment, since smoking is prohibited in so many public places. It was only a few decades ago that people smoked in planes, restaurants, and even movie theaters. Engaging local communities in ways that fit the social landscape can make intervention strategies more successful. This is demonstrated in the adoption of a technology, such as malaria nets, and also in more culturally entrenched behaviors, such as the reduction of multiple sexual partner relationships in Uganda, which is particularly striking in a country with significant levels of polygyny.

THE IDEA AND THE VIRUS

We already take for granted that Google can reveal both the popularity of ideas, people, and themes of all sorts across the globe (through mentions of a subject in on- and offline media) and the popularity of what is searched for by the 400 million search queries on the site each day. Like Google's Ngrams tool, Google Trends offers a great means of tracking the spread of interest in an idea or a health concern in a way that is directly applicable to our model. Let's take as an example the swine flu scare in the spring of 2009. By April 19, 2009, ten days from the initial diagnosis of the H1N1 virus in Mexico, there were a handful of cases, mainly in the United States. Then, on April 22, almost immediately after the Mexican government announced the problem, the "mind virus" cascaded across the borders of North America to all corners of the world, whereas the medical virus was almost absent (or confirmed to have spread only to Scotland, New Zealand, Spain, and Germany). The World Health Organization (WHO) announced a pandemic level 5 alert on April 28, and within forty-eight hours Google searches for swine flu had spread to every country on the planet, including the smallest, poorest, and most remote countries.

Over the next ten days, as more cases of the virus were confirmed in Europe, China, and Latin America, as well as in countries closer to the original outbreak, the mind virus continued to propagate and to mutate rapidly. Even the name used to describe the virus became a mixture of "swine/pig/Mexican flu" and "H1N1." As the human hands and mouths that transmitted the mind virus did their work, all kinds of weird mutations came to light. The Egyptian government slaughtered that country's pig population over fears that infections might spread through the mere presence of the animal supposed to be the cause of the outbreak. The Chinese government either turned away or quarantined Mexicans entering the country, regardless of whether they displayed signs of illness. Pork sales in the United States dropped by more than a quarter.

This is a classic example of an informational cascade, with all of the characteristics of Darwinian evolution—*variation* in the names given to H1N1, *transmission* from person to person(s), both online and face-to-face, and *selection*, when much of the populace reacted to official statements issued by governments or by the WHO. In this case, much of what happened was dominated by transmission. The idea of swine flu spread so rapidly that it reached all corners of the globe before rational selection or much mutation had occurred. This was a remarkable demonstration of rapid social influence that may well have affected the spread of the disease itself, as people became more vigilant or fearful about their own symptoms, restricted their travel, sought immunizations, took hygienic precautions, and so on.

Google Trends data on searches for "swine flu" reflect, at the population level, the relative degree that people searched for the topic independently. As one might expect, the frequency of searches in April–May 2009 had, like the trends we have already considered, a much larger copying parameter than it did an individual learning parameter, but relative to other social phenomena such as academic buzzwords, the selection parameter was actually fairly high. This was presumably a result of genuine public concern driven by the media portrayal of swine flu. This implies that providing information centrally—through the WHO, conventional media outlets, health centers, and the like—had a significant effect, at least on a minority, which is the key to instigating a social cascade, as we saw in the Samsø example.

Contrast this with the bird flu scare of late 2005, which began with almost pure social learning. Interest built up to a peak on October 17 and then fell away steadily in symmetrical form. Then, suddenly, there was a rapid surge in searches for "bird flu," which peaked on November 2 and subsequently declined steadily to the end of the year. Why was there almost pure imitation in September and October, followed by almost pure independent decision? It turns out that on November 1, President George Bush publicly announced his $7 billion "Bird Flu Strategy," with a large amount of publicity. Apparently, an American president is one of the few figures who can spark enough importance or reaction to bring about a collective *independent* response to a problem.

Providing centralized information, such as when the WHO issues announcements, should be more effective for cases where the public is selecting that information based on its intrinsic value. If, on the other hand, the public is receiving information mainly through copying, then the strategy should be to "plant many seeds," particularly in the form of visible behavior—erecting inoculation tents in public spaces or perhaps handing out buttons that people can wear after having been inoculated.

HEARD THAT NAME BEFORE?

So far we have considered phenomena that come and go quickly, such as buzzwords or interest in the spread of particular life-threatening disease. We can see similar patterns over the longer term, but at a certain time scale we need to start thinking of populations as a *flux* of people rather than as a fixed, closed set of individuals. A good example is the popularity of baby names. Names are interesting things. As Harvard psychologist Steven Pinker put it in his book *The Stuff of Thought*, the modern, free choice of a name "encapsulates the great contradiction in human social life: between the desire to fit in and the desire to be unique." The U.S. Social Security Administration provides an incredible online database of baby names, with the kind of data quality and precision that could only be dreamed of in other studies of behavioral change. The database is a detailed record of change over a long period and provides the percentage popularity of the top one thousand baby names for girls and boys for every year for more than a century.

Baby names by their nature are discretely countable—a baby is given a name only once, and it is always clear exactly what that name is. Compare this to the uncertainty of some other less discrete behaviors, such as fidgeting. (As Tony Soprano asked his son's school psychologist, "What constitutes a fidget?") It is clear from studies, not to mention common experience, that a minority of people are original with their names, whereas the majority choose names socially. For example, using historical birth records, one study meticulously showed that when Irish people moved to England in the nineteenth century, the immigrant generation of Paddys and Marys named their boys William, George, and other "standard" English names so that the kids would fit into English society.

Jonah Berger of the Wharton Business School and Stanford University's Gaël Le Mens recently looked at the comings and goings of the top one thousand baby names over the past century and found that, generally speaking, the faster a name rose in popularity, the faster it declined. This was a very nice result, and it matches the social learning version of the model we have been describing, where the rise and decline are nearly symmetrical. Provocatively, Berger and Le Mens described it not in a social sense but in an individual, psychological sense. They explained that the symmetry in rise and decline resulted from people's intuitive sense of what names are "in" and what names are becoming passé.

This conclusion highlights a central question of this book: how much does change on the mass population scale owe to what goes on between our ears rather than between us and others around us? We often believe we know the trends of fashion and control our responses to them, but often our "original" ideas—for a name, a word, a behavior—are actually already becoming popular. Berger and Le Mens argue that people are conscious of naming fashions and jump on the rising wave and avoid what has peaked and begun to decline. This appeals to our individual sense of self-determination, but is it likely? Names have vastly different popularity life spans. Many come and go from the top-thousand within several years—Autry, Trula, and Izora—whereas others stay around much longer—John and Mary were the most popular names for nearly the entire twentieth century. For the individual psychology explanation, we would somehow have to keep track of these vastly different rates of change and *collectively* make our choices accordingly, so that the rate of decline today mirrored the rate of decline of, say forty or fifty years before.

Even if we could do this, how would we get the information? The ubiquitous popularity lists we have online these days are only a recent phenomenon. To get the information would require that each individual American accurately assess the relative popularity of names in the United States, based on local information and his or her own idiosyncratic life experience. That individual minds could manage all these complex calculations seems highly unlikely, and that they would be doing so subconsciously, and in a coordinated fashion to form the national rise-and-decline pattern seems all but impossible.

The alternative is just so much simpler: *we copy names from other people*. Take the particular examples that Berger and Le Mens invoke to show the smooth up-down pattern—Charlene, Kristi, and Tricia. As shown in the figure that follows, the traditional social influence model fits the patterns of these names very well. The rate of adoption increases initially, reaches a peak, and then declines as the cumulative number of adopters asymptotically approaches the saturation limit. Remember that with the yearly popularity of names for new babies, we look at the number of new additions per year. The saturation point simply reminds us that there is a finite number of Americans who will name their girls Kristi or Charlene.

Notice the offset in dates between the peak popularity of the two names. This results, surely, from generations tending to define themselves against one another by avoiding names from the previous generation. This, then, is a psychological explanation—that people are generally aware of names that sound like the older generation—but certainly a plausible one, and a far cry from the kind of sophisticated calculations and omniscience that would underlie any individual's sense of the slope of the popularity curve over years past.

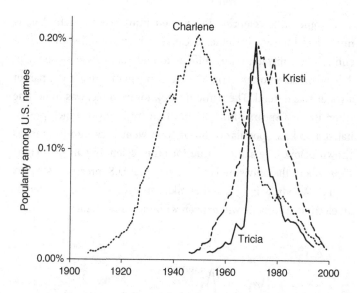

The simple copying model gives us an opportunity to do what we do repeatedly in this book: identify a pattern that does *not* quite fit the model and is therefore interesting as an anomaly. For example, the name Tricia jumped abruptly from 0.05 percent popularity in 1968 to 0.17 percent in 1969—a huge increase compared to other top-thousand names for any period. It is such exceptions from the traditional model that warrant a unique explanation; in this case, presumably Richard Nixon's election as U.S. president in 1968, as his elder daughter's name is Tricia (Patricia).

As much as this "celebrity effect" sounds as if it could be generalized to explain lots of other apparent anomalies, it is vastly more unusual than you might think. Celebrities may be famous—otherwise they wouldn't be celebrities—but their influence on each of us is much less than we imagine. Because names are inherently social entities, in reality it is rather difficult to find examples of a strong, independent selection pattern. Most celebrity names tend to be part of a wider social trend. The name Britney, for example, was in decline when Britney Spears's first album came out in 1999, which precipitated a spike in popularity, but it soon went back into decline, as shown below. The same is true for other celebrity names such as Elvis. About the only sure bet is an unusual U.S. president's name, such as Woodrow in 1912 and Franklin in 1932, which is boosted by an election. The same will happen with the name Barack.

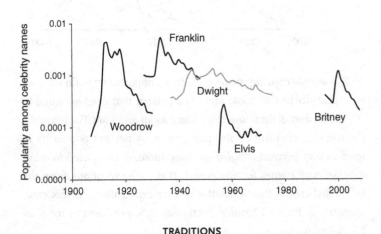

TRADITIONS

In these examples we can get away with using the classic diffusion model, which assumes a fixed population, but often the flux from new generations means that the basic model does not quite work. Consider a rather arcane hobby focused on the windy high-lands of Scotland, where a very particular niche of people has the goal of walking to the top of every Scottish hill over three thousand feet high, which is known as "compleating" (that's their spelling of it) the Munros. Munro compleating became popular through much of the twentieth century, but then the number of new people com-pleating leveled out in the late 1990s. The standard diffusion model we've mentioned does not account for this leveling out in the *rate*—new compleaters per year—of walkers. New young people are con-tinually entering this activity, even if it doesn't get any more popular relative to the total population. As economist Paul Ormerod (an avid Munros compleater) found out, we need only to allow for this con-tinual flux of new young people over time to explain the Munros pattern. Compleating the Munros is a *tradition*, passed from one generation of active hill walkers to the next.

Traditions help define a society because they are created by a copying mechanism that keeps things the same. Anthropologists love traditions for that very reason: they become defining charac-teristics that can be used to distinguish one society from another. We say, for example, that societies X and Y have different marriage traditions, or that societies A and B make their arrow points in dif-ferent ways. Traditions are built on long-term individual learning, in the sense we defined earlier, often through apprenticeship—daugh-ters learning from mothers, sons learning from fathers—in acts of copying repeated over long periods, from early childhood through adolescence. If we call this transmission "vertical," traditions are learned "obliquely" as well. By hanging around the local barber-shop on a Saturday afternoon, a boy of the last century would pick up social cues about how to act in a small U.S. town. Likewise, by hanging around with the males in his kinship group, a Hopi boy in the American Southwest learns the ins and outs of rituals and ceremonies.

Traditions evolve through small differences in the normal routines, which can arise from outside influence, but also through "copying error"—"reading" a recipe incorrectly. Maybe someone notes that the new product is better and begins to reproduce it, passes the information to someone else, who also passes it on, perhaps tinkering with it first. At some point, the new product may become "traditional."

People can then pick and choose among the products. This is *cultural selection*. After a time, some products go extinct whereas others become more plentiful, as manufacturers make more of them to meet demand. This is cultural evolution of the slow, gradual kind. What if the variants are reproduced so fast that selection doesn't have time to operate? Such high, sustained rates—a.k.a. "cascades"—can be just as important to cultural evolution as selection, as we will see in the next chapter.

Before we do, however, let's return for a moment to the tale that started the chapter—the story of Søren Hermannen and Samsø's *social* diffusion of sustainable energy. Social diffusion happens all the time in the world around us—so much so that our language is filled with phrases like "spread like wildfire," "ahead of the curve," and "waves" of change. To be honest, we still find it remarkable that however well known this kind of phenomenon is, much of public policy, traditional social science, and marketing is built on ideas of self-determining individuals shaping their own behavior independently of their peers.

This is particularly perplexing when biologists have shown that the collective motions of flocks or schools can be explained mainly through each bird or fish following its nearest neighbors. Fish can be induced to swim toward a target by introducing a single individual (a robotic fish in the experiments) that influences the direction, not by some macho leadership behavior, complicated signaling, or inherent influence but through his or her consistency of direction, which is picked up and diffused through the school by the action of its members following each other. By following each other, they follow the leader only indirectly. They need not even know who the leader is, just as we do not know who the first person was to text "OMG!" or name a boy Logan. These diffusion patterns can be replicated by very simple diffusion models, so why can't we use this to make the world a giant Samsø? Disappointingly, as we will see in the next chapter, knowing how a cascade works doesn't mean knowing exactly where and when to trigger it.

5

CASCADES

In January 2010, a twenty-seven-year-old accountant from northern England, Paul Chambers, was planning a trip to meet an Irish woman—"@crazycolours"—whom he had met and wooed online. Romantic bliss, it seemed, was just a short flight across the Irish Sea, but that cold, snowy January day proved unusual for Chambers, life-changing even. Exasperated that he might miss out on future happiness because snowy conditions had closed Robin Hood airport, Chambers posted a message to @crazycolours on his Twitter account, saying that if the airport didn't open soon, he would blow it "sky high!!" In his haste, Chambers accidentally sent this message to the 650 others who followed him on Twitter, and, one thing leading to another, he was arrested for the bomb threat. Chambers contended it was all a joke, but the trial judge was not amused, describing his message as "menacing in its content and obviously so. . . . Any ordinary person reading this would see it in that way and be alarmed," as *The Guardian* reported in November 2010. Chambers's one moment of frustration got him fired from his job, a reputation-damaging conviction, and a crushing fine.

In a Hollywood film, this is when something miraculous happens, such as an upwelling of popular support for the little guy, who is being bullied by the state. Actually, this *is* what happened, when, on the eve of Chambers's appeal of his conviction, another Twitter user posted, "I think we should all tweet Paul Chambers's original joke, Spartacus style. Thousands of us. Would that work?" That Twitter user then re-tweeted Chambers's original posting, with a hashtag at the end—"#iamspartacus." This told other Twitter users to rebel Spartacus-style, as in the 1960 film in which all the rebel Roman gladiators show their solidarity with him by proclaiming "I am Spartacus!"

In a blink, this message spread across the Internet as sympathizers both famous and unknown, technophiles and civil-rights campaigners, Brits and Americans, all joined in and copied the message, adding their own variations along the way. This simple expression of support cascaded across Twitter and other social-media platforms and out into the world of newspapers and television. Unfortunately for Chambers, this show of support had no effect on his appeal.

UNINTENDED CASCADES

The success of the #iamspartacus cascade is what marketers, managers of political campaigns, and politicians dream of: the rapid spread of an idea or behavior through a population as a result of the action of its initiator. It's crucial to recognize the lottery-like nature of a cascade. Who could have predicted the #iamspartacus cascade beforehand? Most ideas that we want to spread don't, and Paul Chambers had not actually tried to start anything with his message. Cascades are much more often unintended consequences.

Take the edict issue by the U.K. Department of Education that universities measure the "impact" of the academic research they conduct. Unfortunately, no one really knows what "impact" is, beyond being a rather fuzzy concept that looks at how research publications stack up against each other, or make a difference for "real-world" problems. That doesn't mean the word isn't important. In fact, far from it, as levels of government support are tied to it. End up near the bottom of the impact ranking, and your university could lose millions in funding, which might force program closures, faculty layoffs, and the like. There's a lot riding on that one little word.

Recall from chapter 4 that a buzzword that has some discernible quality to it—as "impact" has, because the U.K. government says it does—can spread through a fortuitous combination of independent learning and social learning, or copying. Imagine all the committees being established to address the future "impact" of universities and their departments. Without a clear definition of what impact is, a lot of the decisions could very well be made in the dark.

That is what this chapter is about: what happens when a choice must be made but it is not apparent what the best option is? In an environment of social influence, if the decision criteria are less than objective, the choices that proliferate can be unpredictable, *cascading* without warning or clear direction through the community.

"IMPACT" CASCADES

As word of the impact focus cascaded through universities, it picked up speed and began to evolve and branch. Along the way, it mutated, like the secret in a Chinese whispers game, so that individuals and nodes of individuals—departments, research groups—created their own ideas of what impact means. (On a much longer time scale, this not so different from how languages with a common origin, such as the Romance languages, diverge over the centuries.) With their academic output—research papers and books—to be graded simply by a summary rating of zero to four stars, professors were rightly concerned. Will my academic peers cite my research? Will it be reported in the news? Understandably, such concerns about "impact" can shift priorities from the research itself—making discoveries—to the more immediate personal goal of publishing widely cited or popular articles, and thus securing one's position.

As economist John Kay describes in *Obliquity*, excessive focus on staying ahead tends to be counterproductive. It can actively inhibit competitiveness, such as when Boeing focuses solely on profits. As age-old sayings like "keep your eye on the ball" imply, it's a pretty simple principle, yet forgotten in overzealous focus on success metrics (scoreboards, star ratings, popularity, impact) that could jeopardize what academia was all about in the first place—exploring knowledge. Rating academic research with a set of stars reflects the common misconception that by actively sorting for things with specific intrinsic qualities, we can shape the landscape and predetermine outcomes. Governments can give this process a boost by assigning "fitness" scores, to borrow a term from evolutionary science, and bringing the highest-scoring research to the fore, trimming away the perceived "fat" in the process.

For Kay—and his inspiration, the philosopher Isaiah Berlin, who in turn was inspired by Leo Tolstoy—this is a "hedgehog" strategy. A hedgehog is close to our individual learner: he knows one thing very well, he sticks to it, and he drives relentlessly toward the goal. The fox is essentially the social one: he knows many things more superficially but is conscious of the limits of his knowledge and continually adapts to new information. The fox strategy is better suited to a complex, ever-changing world, even if we find hedgehogs more convincing. The world is friendlier to foxes than it is to hedgehogs because it is a world of many choices—of similar or hard-to-distinguish quality—existing on a social landscape of *other people*, and lots of them.

NOT SOLID GROUND

When we think about cascades of ideas and behavior—books on investing, the latest in home gadgetry, or healthy lifestyles—we tend to envisage the social landscape through which these ideas spread as *firm ground*, often as a *fixed* social network. What in reality are transient interactions and relationships—a conversation, a schoolmate, or a co-worker—are now so often portrayed as if they were fixed "wires" between people in online social networks. It's as if we were cocooned in a fixed lattice of gooey incubators in *The Matrix*. Those who picture this fixed network of wires between us are excited to launch their idea across it through careful, strategic placement, to get it to spread on its own, say, from one Facebook page to another.

Malcolm Gladwell's *The Tipping Point* convinced people that ideas can spread into every corner as long as we can map the social network and find those "hubs," those "influentials," who sit at the center of social networks. Find the "influential"—a break dancer under a bridge, the creator of a hip new blog, maybe a parkour expert in Paris—and you need to convert only that one key person to set the idea spinning in all directions, from the influential's connections to his or her connections, and so on. The subtitle of market research gurus Ed Keller and Jonathan Berry's *The Influentials: One American in Ten Tells the Other Nine How to Vote, Where to Eat, and What to Buy*—reveals the marketing bestseller to be the latest version of this line of thought.

It is certainly true that all kinds of things spread through social networks. In *Connected*, Nicholas Christakis and James Fowler give plenty of examples of behaviors spreading through social networks—paranoia in communities or even the giggles, which spread over a period of weeks in Africa without anything being funny. It is all too easy, however, to mistake the network metaphor for a rather more fluid and messy reality. When we join in the fashion for network analogies, we tend to forget that the social landscape is dynamic, that for most humans living today, social interactions and relationships are mostly fleeting and multifarious. Unlike the small kinship-based social networks that shaped the lives of our ancestors, the social networks in which most modern humans are embedded are in constant flux.

What's more, even if the social network stays the same, which it doesn't, of course, *everyone else* is also trying to spread his or her ideas the same way. It's like shouting across Times Square on New Year's

Eve. Most of our attempts to spread our ideas or to generate attention for them fail because, as Charles Darwin realized upon reading
Thomas Malthus's essay on population and food supplies, there is
only limited space for success. Hindsight is 20/20, so we look back,
trying to emulate past successes that no one predicted beforehand,
no matter how lucky or complex or timely those past successes were.
We try to adapt our new efforts to align them with what we perceive
worked in the past, but this almost never succeeds. For one thing,
we are not at the same point in history. Social influence might still
be strong at the local scale but lead to unpredictable consequences at
larger scales. How do we make our way through this changing landscape? How do we become more fox and less hedgehog?

THINGS GET COMPLEX

It helps to accept that uncertainty is natural. The *New Scientist* had
on its March 2010 cover the "radical" notion that biological evolution can be unpredictable. To biologists, this was not news. Back in
the 1960s, population geneticists Motoo Kimura and James Crow
had introduced the neutral theory of evolutionary drift to account for
the unpredictability of evolution. Their theory held that the majority of evolutionary changes we see at the molecular level are caused
by random drift of selectively neutral mutations. "Selectively neutral" refers to a mutation that does not affect the fitness of the individual or individuals possessing it, and the term can apply equally as
well to behaviors. If, for example, we don't select mates on the color
of their hair, then hair color is a neutral trait. To some, it appeared
that Kimura and Crow's theory flew in the face of Darwin's evolution

by means of natural selection, but it soon became clear that the two evolutionary processes, selection and drift (neutrality), were complementary, not competitive.

Later, in the 1990s, the unpredictability of evolution again assumed center stage with the entrance of complexity theory. Interest in complexity was boosted by a small number of talented academicians from physics, economics, biology, and archaeology at the Santa Fe Institute in New Mexico. In its early days, as today, there was a mixture of the concrete and the fuzzy emanating from the institute. The former comprises the nuts and bolts of physical phenomena—what they look like, what their components are, and such—whereas the latter comprises some of the complex interactions among phenomena, many highly theoretical and some downright speculative.

Murray Gell-Mann fascinated us with fuzzy phenomena in his book *The Quark and the Jaguar*. He wrote that scientists were hard at work trying to understand how complex structures emerge from quite simple rules that govern interactions among their component parts. When Santa Fe Institute researchers said "simple rules," they meant it. Physicists were modeling people as polarized magnets in a lattice, either "up" or "down." When you reverse the polarity of one person, it might cause an adjacent person to flip that way and cause a chain reaction that resembles the cascading change of direction in a herd of cattle.

One of the leading thinkers in the early days of the institute was Stuart Kauffman, who was working on the problem of modeling a system of interacting agents in which each agent's actions depend on those of other agents. Kauffman revitalized population geneticist

Sewall Wright's powerful 1930s concept of the fitness landscape—a theoretical landscape filled with peaks and valleys that correspond to a set of choices open to an organism, each of which affects its fitness either positively (peaks) or negatively (valleys).

Kauffman added the time dimension to model what he called the "dynamic" fitness landscape. For each individual embedded in a network of interrelations, actions depend not only on the interaction rules assigned to the individual, but also on the individual's interactions with all other agents in its communication network. Given that the actions of the neighbors change continually, optimal strategies are only approximate in the present because they depend on the previous actions of other agents, which will be different in the next moment. This calls to mind what evolutionary biologist Leigh van Valen termed the "Red Queen effect," whereby an organism must keep changing just to stay competitive, just as the Lewis Carroll character had to keep running faster just to remain in the same place.

Kauffman showed that if agents are only moderately connected, then they can all adapt to each other fairly easily—there is a Mount Fuji that all can climb, as when the Hunt brothers bought all the silver they could back in the 1980s (only to lose their shirts as the price plummeted). As things become more interconnected, the landscape becomes more rugged and dynamic. Agents can make small adjustments to optimize their current strategy or risk a big jump to a nearby peak, that is, to a better long-term strategy. When the network is completely interconnected, the landscape is so rugged and undulating that highly favorable strategies no longer exist and a directed search for improvement is no better than random guessing, such as when everyone else becomes cognizant of changing silver prices. What got everyone excited about Kauffman's model was that it produced avalanches of change of all sizes, mostly small but occasionally very large, as a system hovered between an ordered regime of stasis and a chaotic regime of unpredictable change—a state "poised at the edge of chaos," as Kauffman famously put it.

WHEN POWER LAWS CASCADED

Kauffman's model also demonstrates the widespread fascination at that time with inverse power laws, a particular distribution of phenomena that is unlike the classic bell curve, or normal distribution, with its well-defined mean and easily calculable standard deviation. Since then, statisticians have pointed out that pure power laws, like diamonds, are rare and pristine, and so it's safer (they tend to get heated about this) just to refer more generally to "long tail" distributions. The popularity of girls' names, as we show in the chart that follows, has a long tail and no meaningful average. Wealth is another long-tailed distribution; economist Vilfredo Pareto's observation in 1906 that 80 percent of the land in Italy was held by only 20 percent of the population is commonly referred to as the "80/20 rule."

There was a mystical quality to power laws in those days, inspiring for many. You could take a data set for a series of events or phenomena—the sizes of earthquakes, the irregularities of the heartbeat, word frequencies in English—and either rank order them in terms of size or frequency or create a histogram of their sizes, and the result would be a magical, elegant distribution like the one that follows. If you plotted the data with the axes showing orders of magnitude (powers of ten, say), the result would appear as a (nearly) straight

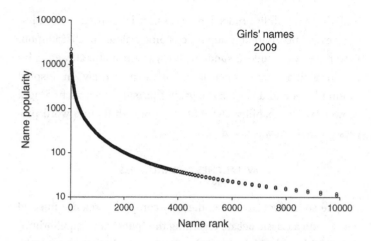

line. To look at the smoothness of the straight line, which emerged from an apparent random assortment of data, made it seem as if a new hidden order was being revealed by nature itself. The potential seemed awesome, as it was easy to see the analogy with human society, with its inherent interconnections among people, organizations, and regulations and where avalanches of change were fresh in the minds of the post–cold war, dot-com population.

This was part of a larger cascade in the 1990s, a frenzied rush of discoveries of "power law" distributions (some rather dubious, it must be said) in social data—economic markets, the then still new World Wide Web, Hollywood actor networks, and university research funding. Marketers were not immune to this fashion. "Direct-response" marketers—those using mail and other direct-response media—jumped aboard the trend to justify the way they valued certain customer groups without acknowledging the

underlying instability. Indeed, many asserted the "fixed" and endur-
ing location of different groups of customers along the distribution.
Power laws were indeed suddenly everywhere, and it all went a bit
too far, with a *Nature* paper describing a "power law" in hospital
waiting lines and arcane navel-gazing pursuits such as finding a
"power law" probability distribution of line shifts in a word pro-
cessor when text was inserted.

AVALANCHES AND WILDFIRES

Despite some overeagerness, the new complexity science injected
energy into a classic debate regarding the "punctuated equilibrium"
described by paleobiologists Niles Eldredge and Stephen J. Gould.
The debate was over whether fossil species extinctions were somehow interconnected not through extreme external events (such as
an asteroid impact) but rather through small triggering events cascading through the vast tangle of ecological interdependency among
species. A prevailing analogy was to think of evolution as being like
a pile of sand, with more sand slowly being poured onto the peak.
Usually the grains land without much disturbance, but occasionally
one grain can trigger a massive sandslide. Like the addition of a grain
of sand to the sandpile, the extinction of a single species could cause
the extinction of other species that are ecologically dependent on it.

According to the late Danish theoretical physicist Per Bak, both
evolution and sandpiles exhibit "self-organized criticality"—a property of systems that are in continual flux but precariously balanced
between the buildup of interdependencies. In sandpiles and evolution, change occurs intermittently rather than smoothly and gradu-

ally. "Critical" points are reached, which trigger bursts, or avalanches, that extend over a wide range of magnitudes.

The analogy of the sandpile was a seductive start, but Bak and
his colleague Kim Sneppen made the model even simpler and in
the process more satisfying. They modeled an "ecosystem" through
the arrangement of index numbers ("species") in a circle, such that
each agent interacted with its two nearest neighbors. Each agent was
represented by a fitness value between 0 and 1, chosen at random to
start the simulation. Their simulation then ran in a series of steps.
At each time step, the lowest fitness value in the circle was selected
against and assigned a new random value. The two nearest neighbors of the chosen agent were also randomly assigned new fitness
values, equaling the "adaptation" of dependent agents. It was all so
simple. At each time step in the simulation, the smallest fitness,
together with the fitnesses of the two neighbors, were replaced with
new random fitnesses. The step was repeated again and again. And
from this there seemed to unravel a secret of the complex universe.
Bak even titled his popular book *How Nature Works,* and Kauffman
theologized this sentiment in his book *Reinventing the Sacred: A New
View of Science, Reason, and Religion.*

Through selection against the worst fitness in each time step, the
fitnesses of all remaining agents rise over time. At some point, the
ecosystem becomes poised for an avalanche. All the species are fit,
but according to the rules, one of them gets removed in the next step.
As soon as one of the species goes, it takes a couple of others with
it, and all of those are replaced by random values, which more than
likely are less than the fitness values of the majority of other agents.
Often, one of these newest replacements will be chosen again, and

so on, as a localized avalanche forms. This is like a championship football team from which one player retires, and management keeps trying to replace that player with untested, mediocre players who make their teammates play badly as well, so they too get canned, and soon much of the once great team has been replaced.

Bak and Sneppen found that the sizes of the avalanches—the number of species taken out by a single triggering event—followed a true power law distribution. In other words, the toy model, in all its simplicity, seemed to replicate patterns of the evolutionary history of the Earth. Soon afterward, physicist Mark Newman contested this model with a model of his own, which produced almost the same power law of extinction sizes but without any interconnections. Decades later, this is less important than how Bak and Sneppen started people thinking about how massive avalanches of extinctions could occur through internal changes only, with small changes poising the system continually for a possible massive avalanche at any time.

"Like wildfire," you might say. Geologist Donald Turcotte and his colleagues, for example, found that forest fires, in terms of the number of trees that burn, are distributed by a power law. They built a model that assumed that trees were added in random places to a spatial grid and that every now and then a "match" was dropped into a random square of the grid. If the match fell on a square with a tree, the tree would burn and adjacent trees would also catch fire. After trees had been accumulating for a while without a big fire, they would find themselves in a massive interconnected cluster, poised for a big fire from a future match. Massive fires were rare within a genuine power law distribution of modeled forest fires that virtually matched the distribution of real forest fires over time. Turcotte and David Roberts later applied the forest fire analogy to armed conflicts. Most small skirmishes are squashed, but occasionally there is the Boston Massacre of 1775, or the assassination of Archduke Ferdinand of Austria in 1914, or the felling of the Twin Towers in New York in 2001, which sparks considerably more armed conflict.

CASCADES IN HIGHLY CONNECTED NETWORKS

Duncan Watts, currently director of the Human Social Dynamics group at Yahoo!, was a doctoral student at Cornell in the nineties and became interested in how ideas cascade through social networks. He modeled a random but fixed network of agents, very much like the forest fire model but with the crucial difference of making the "trees" more like people. Following a famous 1950s psychology experiment by Solomon Asch, Watts introduced thresholds of conformity, where agents would change behavior only when a certain fraction of their "friends" had. His model had each agent represented by a zero at the start, then one agent was given an "idea" by switching it to a one. At the next time step, another randomly selected agent would be switched from zero to one. These randomly selected agents were the innovators.

Agents were assigned threshold values representing how much peer pressure it would take for them to change opinion. A threshold of 0.85, for example, meant that an agent would adopt an idea once 85 percent of his or her friends had adopted it. Each time an agent switched, that changed the friend's circle for all surrounding agents and might cause one of them to switch, and so on, leading to a cascade. Of course, cascades occur more readily through a network of agents with low thresholds than with high ones. If the thresholds are too high, then system-sweeping avalanches become practically impossible, with each avalanche ultimately being curtailed by particularly stubborn agents.

Watts also found that a sparsely connected, scale-free network is subject to cascades of all sizes (through a power law distribution), but as random connections are added, the size of the cascades becomes limited, such that small changes build up until suddenly a single, massive cascade occurs all at once. The reason for this is that most agents in a sparsely connected network have only a few direct neighbors and are therefore susceptible to change from a single neighbor, whereas in a highly connected network a single friend out of many is less likely to surpass the tipping point. Just as Kauffman and Bak found, it appears that as agents become more highly interconnected, they are overwhelmed with information and are less likely to make a bold decision.

This is why it is so important to consider interconnections that change all the time when we try to understand social cascades. It can be tempting to apply analogies rooted in physical models, especially when we talk about ideas "spreading like wildfire" or refer to the advice of Watts to "light many fires." The crucial thing here, which is sometimes lost in the analogy, is that there is no way of knowing where the match should be dropped. When you deal with people and their ephemeral interactions, there is no two-dimensional grid of flammable trees that we can scrutinize to find the tip of the giant, interconnected cluster. Only in hindsight can we see that a spread of ideas happens when society is poised for it. A big idea might be invented at one time, to little response, and then years later get invented again, often without credit being given to the first instance, and become a big splash. Plate tectonics changed geology only in the 1960s, decades after Alfred Wegener and Arthur Holmes had described continental drift in the early twentieth century, when few people were paying attention.

Another related question is, what generally makes a system poised for a cascade? One of the lubricants is a variation in the agents in the network. As we described in chapter 3, social diffusion is made easier when there are at least a few agents who choose individually and others who amplify those decisions through social imitation. This variability is a key aspect. When Watts introduced a range of different thresholds to the agents—such that some were innovators, others early adopters, others late majority, and so on—system-sweeping cascades became more likely. There was a mix of early adopters (low threshold) to get the cascade started and early and late majority agents to keep it going.

TREES, AGAIN

Once it has occurred, every cascade has a definite series of events, of one change leading to another change or multiple changes, and so on, which we could, in theory, track as a tree of interconnected events, in much the same way as we construct evolutionary trees. At the base is the seminal idea (trunk), which gives rise to several spin-off ideas (large branches), which in turn give rise to other, less significant (or more specialized) spin-off ideas (smaller branches), and so on, until another new seminal idea starts a new avalanche (new tree). This tree of ideas could be seen growing in time and spreading into more and more remote corners of contemporary culture. If branch lengths were drawn in proportion to how influential—how often copied—each idea was, the depiction of a "tree of ideas" might take on a *fractal* form, much like the recursive trees we showed in chapter 3. Like a river system, which looks the same at its largest scale right down to its tributaries and then to the small-scale rivulets of water draining through the sand on a beach, a fractal is said to be *self-similar*, if not identical, at all scales.

As a model, a growing fractal tree combines aspects of cascades with the process of evolution. Picture the tree such that only the tips represent living agents, or active ideas, and the vertices represent agents or ideas that have since been replaced or become extinct. The distance between two events can be represented as the distance back to the first common ancestor. What would happen if, as the fractal tree evolved, branches were pruned so that surviving branches became isolated and no longer affected any neighbors when they mutated? Think of the "self-organized criticality" model and all its sweeping implications, and how in time some researchers were claiming they had found self-organized criticality in the way line breaks cascaded in word-processed texts. The idea spreads to all corners, getting smaller with every turn, just as a fractal river network erodes upstream and fills the landscape with smaller and smaller tributaries.

Economist Brian Arthur has argued that technology builds on itself in this fractal pattern through a repeated process of existing technologies being combined as parts of newer technologies. We can actually track this in the academic world because each publication cites in its bibliography (or is supposed to) all the previous articles that have influenced it. What eventually happens? We get a classic silo effect and the creation of more isolated projects. As these proliferate, the number of researchers interested in any particular result gets smaller and smaller, although the number of results, and the number of researchers, continues to increase.

Is it any wonder that at some point an outside force, perhaps the government, steps in and tries to guide things by, for example by taking account of the "impact" that these products have? Or a new CEO steps in and says that his automobile company has lost its way and needs to immediately reorganize the lines of cars that today's consumers want? In both cases, it is undoubtedly easier said than done. As much as the U.K. government might wish it so, examining impact in and of itself will not cause a unified movement toward better research being conducted at its universities. Instead, it will cause a cascade of ways to *portray* things as having an impact, regardless of whether they do. This, in our view, will lead, by means of the fractal branching pattern, to different and still more siloed views of impact at each university. The bottom line is, you can't simply legislate cascades. They either happen or they don't, but as with evolution in general or the trees and powerful rivers that are often provide the basis for our nature-based metaphors, you can't just will something to change course.

LEARNING FROM CASCADES

Cascades are very much like the diffusion we described in chapter 4 in that a variant can diffuse across a population and can do so widely.

That said, studies of cascades often specify how the individuals are interconnected and what the individual thresholds to change are. In his cascade model, Duncan Watts used a random network and a general threshold for "peer pressure." Technically, a cascade might be predicted on one of these toy models, but the problem is that with just a small amount of real-world variability (fluid network, human diversity), cascades become unpredictable.

If cascades are unpredictable, and rather like a lottery, you would be foolish to try to pick a single winner beforehand. Is there any way around this—a way to profit, no matter who wins? One way is to hold the lottery yourself. In talent shows such as "America's Got Talent" and "X Factor," Simon Cowell and co-investors don't try to predict the winner; they just invest in whatever winner the show develops and indeed build that popularity along the way. Holding the lottery and benefiting is generally not fair to the rest of the population, which is the reasoning behind antitrust laws and the basis for creation of the Securities Exchange Commission.

Our goal is not predictability so much as it is general understanding. For example, we often think that ideas spread most rapidly on a dispersed, hub-and-spoke network, but MIT researcher Damon Centola recently found that highly clustered networks (recall our Samsø example from chapter 4) may actually be better at spreading innovations because of a repetition-threshold effect. Clustering of the network allows the same idea to be introduced to individuals repeatedly, from different neighbors in their social network. We may have to face the fact that social change has these general properties while still remaining specifically unpredictable. Let's move on to chapter 6 and examine this prospect further.

6

WHEN IN DOUBT, COPY

In 2008, CNBC stock market analyst Jim Cramer shouted his infamous recommendation into the TV camera: "No, no, no! Bear Stearns is fine! Don't move your money from Bear!" Soon afterward, Bear Stearns went belly up. On the *Daily Show*, comic Jon Stewart said, "If I had only taken CNBC's advice, I would have a million dollars today—provided I started with $100 million." A lot of people made fun of Cramer, including Cramer himself, who apologized profusely to his (former) fans who lost millions.

Cramer has been a great piñata, but there is another way of looking at the issue, as Diane Brady commented in *Business Week*. Cramer, with his many mea culpas, sold himself short by neglecting to point out how many predictions he makes in a year. The Bear

Stearns prediction was a gaffe, and a large one, but that particular one was cherry-picked from the total number of predictions Cramer made. What about all the ones that *didn't* turn out so bad?

The financial meltdown that started in the last half of 2007 and reached epic proportions by late 2008 seems now as if it should have been predicted by anyone who looked at the asset sheets. The U.S. banking system had a liquidity problem as a result of overvalued assets, and the housing bubble was ready to burst. The broad markets were definitely poised for a sell-off, but what would trigger it, and when would it occur? Except perhaps to a few insiders, Bear Stearns was unpredictable as the specific grain of sand that would ultimately trigger the avalanche. Pundits who live on hindsight write as if they could have predicted the collapse of Bear Stearns, Merrill Lynch, Washington Mutual, and other specific investment and financial services businesses if they had just had all the information. But they're probably wrong.

Unpredictability extends far beyond the financial marketplace. As we discussed in chapter 5, it is the essence of biological evolution. "Which groups will ultimately prevail," Darwin wrote in the *Origin*, "no man can predict; for we well know that many groups, formerly most extensively developed, have now become extinct." And as Stephen J. Gould said about evolution in *Wonderful Life*, if we re-run the tape of life, the general effect is the same, but the exact specifics are different and unpredictable. The biological world, then, parallels the marketplace. As Paul Ormerod writes in his book *Why Most Things Fail*, which species live and which ones die, or which companies weather a financial downturn and which ones fail and trigger massive securities sell-offs, can't really be predicted. We might make educated guesses, but over the long haul we'll probably do no better than throwing darts and picking our winners and losers that way. If you want to make money in the stock market, pick an index fund and stick with it. It's no accident that they're called "index" funds.

To see how easily interaction can undo prediction, consider something we normally think of as predictable, such as orbits of the planets in the sky. In the early seventeenth century, Johannes Kepler derived equations to predict the motions of two bodies in orbit around each other—Earth and its moon, for example—but as is well known to undergraduate physics students, a problem with *three* or more bodies—the Sun and all its planets—is not exactly solvable. Astronomers can update the locations of the bodies, and then predict incrementally where they will go next, but they can never predict their motions indefinitely with one overarching equation.

For understanding human social behavior, thinking in terms of two-player games can give us plenty of insights, especially when we have cross-cultural information for comparison. For example, think back to our discussion in chapter 2 of the field experiments conducted by Joe Henrich and his colleagues. How real are these games in terms of what happens in life? Just as the orbits of three planets lack the determinism of two orbits, games with three players are quite different from those with only two. Of course, this doesn't stop us from generalizing from two-body problems, but let's look at a couple of real-world examples with multiple players, not in an attempt to discover some deep governing laws—there aren't any—but to look briefly at the dynamics involved.

EXTENDING THE GAME

No one could have predicted the outcome of the 2010 parliamentary elections in the U.K., in which no party received a majority of votes. On election night there were standing not two but three viable candidates for prime minister—Liberal Democrat candidate Nick Clegg, Labour candidate Gordon Brown, and Conservative candidate David Cameron. The Conservatives had received a plurality of seats in the elections, but they were twenty seats short of a majority, and it was far from clear that they would be able to form a government. This was a three-body problem in a system accustomed to two-body problems. As it turned out, sentiment against the Labour party, which had been in power since 1997, was widespread, and Cameron received Clegg's support and formed the first coalition government since 1974.

Similarly, in the United States the three-person basketball game of Hustle, in which each player tries to score as much as possible against his two opponents, is more complex than one-on-one basketball. Hustle has natural trade-offs between defending the player with the ball and letting the third player do that, while you (pretending to defend) wait for the rebound and try and score. In any multiplayer game, it often pays to let others make their move first, then copy their successes and avoid repeating their failures. The television program *The Apprentice* is a nice showcase for this strategy, which we also find in politics and academia. Real life, however, is not a three-person game, or even a four-person game, and prediction becomes ever more a pipe dream. Our encounters with others are now arenas in which countless all-against-all games are being played at once.

Millions of people try to make their own ideas more popular than yours. Countless ideas compete against each other for our attention, each following a seemingly different path toward hoped-for success in the marketplace. Some ideas may be bright green, some very interesting, some comfortable, some sexy, but most fail to become popular. The few that do become popular often succeed through a run of dumb luck.

LONG TAILS

Wired editor Chris Anderson labeled this endless diversity of choice the "long-tail market," where a few blockbuster ideas are by far the most popular and the vast majority of competitors are out there in the long tail. In chapter 5 we introduced long-tail distributions and the so-called 80/20 rule. Anderson's illustrative example is book sales on Amazon.com, where a few of the top bestsellers can outsell all others—millions of books—farther out in the long tail. The number-one idea may be, say, four times as popular as the number-two idea and nine times as popular as the number-three idea, and so on.

There are so many choices in the long tail—think of the millions of Amazon titles or possible music downloads—that Anderson has argued for a whole new market philosophy, one that spreads the risk across the endless variety of low-volume choices and free, online distribution rather than staking everything on a few blockbuster titles. In this long-tail world, conditions change rapidly and information is incomplete. So many competing, similar options exist in the long tail that independent choice has very little to grab on to—literally hundreds of Scandinavian food cookbooks, thousands of Sudoku volumes and biographies of Benjamin Franklin, and several hundred guides on tomatoes. In the long-tail distribution shown below, retailers have several immediate options for selling books. Physical retailers—your local bookstore, for example—stock fewer titles, but they're the ones that are the most popular. No matter what, a bookstore is going to carry John Grisham's latest release. Hybrid retailers—Barnes and Noble—carry even more titles in stock because they can cover their bets in two ways: putting books on store shelves and also selling them online using a central distribution system. A pure digital retailer such as Amazon.com has the greatest flexibility because it can find just about any title you want through its acquisition network of new and used books.

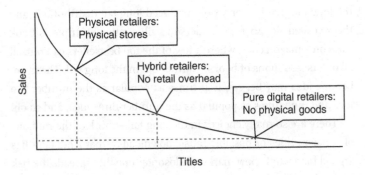

In some ways, this multitude of choices is not necessarily a problem for us. It's not like we are prehistoric people choosing a crucial hunting or fishing strategy, where a wrong choice could lead to death. Quite the opposite; the long-tail market is one of unprecedented frivolity. Now the choice is what book to buy, what to blog about, or what buzzwords to use. We must have chocolate, but should it be Ecuadorian 77 percent dark or Pennsylvanian 76 percent dark? What to have, what to have? Just pick one. There's usually no "wrong" answer.

The marketing scientist Andrew Ehrenberg similarly looked for population-level generalities among all the individual idiosyncrasies in any consumer market. By analyzing sales data directly, Ehrenberg often overturned received wisdom of the "Mad Men" world. In the sixties and seventies he radically maintained that there was no such thing as dependable consumer loyalty, and that advertising could rarely be a strong force in how people made decisions. Repeated analysis of data from a huge range of consumer markets led Ehrenberg and colleagues to develop a model—termed a "Dirichlet," in honor of the nineteenth-century German mathematician—in which it was assumed that consumers had no inherent brand preference and made choices based on chance and availability. If we add to this the newer realizations about social learning, we have the basic ingredients for a certain "interpretive norm," as Ehrenberg put it, or a basic canvas against which more purposeful behavior would stand out.

A key distinction is recognizing the difference between the broader scale, where we select purposefully, and the finer scale, where one choice is about as good as another. It is better to eat than not to eat. That's a broader-scale issue. And as long as you're not diabetic, you can get away, at least in the short run, with subsisting on chocolate. What kind of chocolate to eat? That's a finer-scale issue and not a very important one. Likewise, it probably is a good idea to give your son a name. That's a broader-scale issue because without a name he won't do very well in life. He'll never be admitted to school, and he'll never get a Social Security card or a passport. In fact, he probably won't be released from the hospital so you can take him home. *What* to name him is a separate issue. It probably doesn't make too much difference what you call him, although you would probably want to take Johnny Cash's advice and not call him Sue. If you do, that might elevate things back to the broader scale, where survival is an issue.

What often matters is not which thing is better (for all practical purposes, they're identical) but *who else* is using the thing. You notice someone else's Armani frames, and it later occurs to you that Armani is what you want. You might have copied a behavior subconsciously, or maybe you saw that someone wearing Armanis had better success in attracting dates than someone without them. It doesn't matter whether it was the glasses or something else that gave the person the dating edge. All that matters is that *you* made the logical leap from glasses to success. The bottom line is, we buy the same glasses we saw on someone else; we use that name we heard but can't quite remember when; and we avoid products that "may contain nuts" or are "genetically engineered" for reasons we're not quite sure of. We get so caught up in ideas that are in the air that we tend to lose even the simplest ability for individual thought and reasoning.

COPYCATS

Copying is what people have always done because it's not only easy, it's effective. If it weren't, we wouldn't still be doing it because we wouldn't be here. Our hominin ancestors, who we *know* were

copycats par excellence, would have copied themselves out of existence if it were ineffective. The fact that humans live in groups
and have heightened cognitive abilities ensures that copying has a
revered place in our behavioral arsenal. Not to dwell on the by now
obvious point, but our ability to copy, and to do it so well, was one of
the magnets that drew the three of us into studying the social arena
in the first place. We think of our ancestors in East Africa two million years ago as being "primitive," but it's amazing to see the strong
patterning in the stone tools they made. They all knew what the
other guys were doing because they copied each other. Likewise, pot-
ters in Central Europe seven thousand years ago copied the designs
on each other's pots. Copying is so effective that all sorts of animals,
even fishes, copy each other's behavior in order to adapt. When real
people rather than computers play games, they don't doggedly follow tit-for-tat or some other mechanical algorithm. They copy other
people's winning strategies.

That said, it is striking how negative our culture can be about
copying. Oscar Wilde—the paragon of the creative individualist—
despaired of his run-of-the-mill peers when he observed, "most people's lives are quotations from the lives of others." It is much the
same in behavioral science. Game theorists, for example, call copying "scrounging" or "eavesdropping." Even so, they have been forced
to reconsider the negative connotations after our animal behaviorist colleague Kevin Laland held a computer strategy tournament in
2009. Unlike in Robert Axelrod's one-on-one prisoner's dilemma
games that we looked at in chapter 2, there were pre-set strategies that players could learn from each other. Based on the years
of research following the Axelrod tournament, the winner of the

Laland tournament was expected to exhibit independent rational decision making supplemented by *some* social learning.

As in 1984, however, the results surprised the research community. Not only were the winners graduate students who had never researched the topic before deciding to enter the tournament, the highest-scoring strategies relied heavily on social learning, not on individual experimentation. What put the winner and runner-up ahead of their competitors was their use of memory that was biased toward the most recent observations. Information from observing others long ago was discounted relative to more recent information. What, then, lifted the winner over the runner-up was that the winning strategy not only was biased against older information, it discounted highly variable information even more.

For dynamic social landscapes, the take-home message from the tournament is clear: let others bear the risk of working out what to do, then copy those who succeed and act quickly, so you don't fall behind other copiers. Axelrod and Michael Cohen advised similarly in a business management book, *Harnessing Complexity*: exploit what you've learned immediately, and move even faster if the environment is rapidly changing. In Malcolm Gladwell's terms, just *blink* and take advantage of acting without hesitation or even deliberation. What makes this blink possible? Perhaps a deep-seated instinct, but more often probably just having observed it in someone else—somewhere, sometime—at which point it became lodged in your subconscious.

Subconscious copying is obviously part of language use. Considering words, as we did in chapter 4, rarely can the person who introduced a slang term ever be identified because we copy slang unconsciously, sometimes even imagining that we invented a particular word ourselves. This is why slang is often much older than we think it is. Even many of the Internet slang terms that we see and hear—LOL and L8R, for example—date from the 1980s or before.

Copying is pretty safe, too, since at least you will be doing something that has succeeded to the point of becoming visible to you. The easiest thing to do, even by accident, is to copy something popular and successful. In the social world, popularity *is* success, so you'll be doing fine. Imagine copying the outfit of the last person of your sex whom you met. Even if doesn't seem to be your style, you could get through the day with it, right? You might even like it after trying it out.

If we zoom out and focus on the population scale, we might be able to simplify how we categorize our options. We could simply distinguish *directed* copying, where people direct (or bias) their copying in some advantageous direction, from *undirected* copying, where people copy, perhaps subconsciously, without much knowledge about the person they are copying from. Let's take a look at each of these.

DIRECTED COPYING

For many cases of directed copying, we can exploit the traditional social diffusion models from chapter 3. These have people copying other people, but in many renditions the copying is directed at the behavior or object itself, not at any specific person. To use Kevin Laland's term, these models are based on the "copy if better" rule. Classic diffusion models work best when the new option is a noticeable improvement, as often happens with technology, such as the bow and arrow of prehistoric North America or hybrid corn in the United States in the 1930s. If it *is* a better option, then once the choice finally arrives to you via someone else, you're likely to adopt it, whether it's a tractor over a horse-drawn plow or an iPhone over your old mobile phone.

Classic diffusion models often involve a binary choice: something is either adopted or it is not. In the real world, however, we rarely deal with simple binary options, where one is better than the other. In cases of multiple equivalent options, spreading an idea is not like sending a wave through a placid pond. It is more like confronting a busy swimming pool full of splashing kids. Wherever you look, just about everyone is creating a small wave of his or her own. The pool is rough, dynamic, and unpredictable. How do you explain the spread of ideas through this pool, or the development of different, group-specific social norms?

When confronted with a confusing array of seemingly equivalent options, another way to direct one's copying is toward a particular person rather than trying to choose among all the different objects or behaviors themselves. As for *whom* we copy, there is a vast body of research on the topic, as we saw in chapter 3. We may direct our attention toward prestigious people, people whom we're related to, attractive people, people who are similar to us, popular people, older people, younger people, and so on. This has often been studied in traditional societies, in which kinship, status, and traditional forms of leadership and organization are essential components of influence.

Among these strategies of copying people, perhaps the most useful ones are directed toward people or groups that we're trying to identify with. This is a form of conformity, which can lead to social diffusion within the limits of the group that is conforming. For example, a popular name diffuses through a generation, a dialect diffuses through an ethnic community, or a certain set of interlinked customs diffuses through a community claiming a common identity. In these cases, conformity directs the copying according to the rule of "copy the majority."

The paradox of conformity, of course, is that we are all conformists in some way, and yet we do not all do the same thing—far from it. In fact, we find the greatest diversity of behaviors in places where people are the most densely packed together, such as New York, London, or Istanbul. One reason for this is that we seek different identities, and people like their distinctiveness, so they look for identity in small groups rather than in the masses. Instead of copying the masses, we might copy a known prestigious person. Others in our group will probably copy that same prestigious figure or get their cue from others locally that they should copy that person. In other words, we often seek to conform *locally* rather than globally. When conformity is directed locally, it might mean we adopt something only after enough of our friends or colleagues have adopted it.

The cascade models we discussed in chapter 5 showed how the addition of local neighborhoods, where there are *thresholds* to copying, introduce unpredictability even into simple binary choice models. In this case, it's the network configuration of these interconnected neighbors that determines how far the cascade will go. Unlike the classic diffusion models, in which an idea spreads smoothly and inexorably, a cascade needs an idea to arrive at the right place at the right time. This leads to the stuttering, stop-start nature of cascades—some ideas trigger an avalanche, but most just cause minor ripples. A moment before the tipping point, little is happening. We like to lean back and say, "This situation looks stable!" Then comes the massive cascade. Jim Cramer learned this the hard way, as have countless others.

Conversely, people might conform according to a global threshold, such as choosing something they know is popular. A person might try to go with what he or she perceives as the most popular behavior at all times, or at least choose things predominantly from the top five, a rule that is quite easy to follow in today's world of popularity lists for novels, music, and news stories. Even scientific articles are listed like this. A million people buying the number-one seller at Amazon.com is a very directed form of copying and a very rational form of copying. It is social learning at its most precise and selective.

UNDIRECTED COPYING

The long-tail world of directed copying is a radical departure from traditional societies, not in terms of human nature but in terms of the massive intermingled diversity of choices and motivations for making them. There can just be far too many people to choose from, many as uninformed as you are, and a myriad idiosyncratic reasons you might copy one person or another. In other words, there is not only an exhausting number of similar *things* to choose from, there can be far too many *people,* or even categories of people who look and act similarly, for us to know whom to copy, especially since they are probably copying others as well.

We might try to copy the successful, or the prestigious, but which ones, in a world where so many compete to portray these qualities, and not always honestly? Also, in a world where everyone competes socially and learns socially, our best strategies must also change from one moment to the next. This again is the Red Queen effect applied to people: we need to run faster just to stay in one place, to keep changing just to stay competitive. For all those thousands of little choices we have to make every day—what shoes, what percentage cocoa in our dark chocolate, what viral news story to chat about using which buzzwords—maybe we can just pick someone, virtually anyone, to copy and save a lot of time. Besides, someone else's choice will probably be perfectly acceptable. It works for them, after all.

We can call this *undirected copying*, and it probably applies more to the current world than it ever has, mainly because of choice overload. Many of us might copy in this manner quite unconsciously, or we may copy certain things quite carelessly. Undirected copying, however, can apply as a model even if each person has a specific reason for copying someone else, because at the population level there are so many different idiosyncratic reasons out there that we can *consider* it undirected.

Generally speaking, undirected copying refers to the population scale. It's seeing the forest rather than the trees, to recall the forest fire model of chapter 5, or even more dynamically, like the pressure of air in a tire. Each air molecule has a very specific direction and speed at any given time. Do we care? No. All we care about is whether our tire has air in it. Similarly, when modeling collective behavior, we may be able to overlook all the idiosyncratic, personal reasons people give for their actions, especially if they wind up acting the same in the end.

We can try just *assuming* that undirected copying is the general rule and see what the model produces. If it matches real-world data, then an undirected-copying model can be used to predict rates of change as well as to distinguish between copying and other forms of social behavior. If it doesn't match, this helps identify situations where there *is* some coherent direction of copying—people copying a particular person or a category of people or choosing something with some generally agreed-upon quality.

The undirected-copying model works like this: take a number of individuals and lots of different ideas from which to choose. From one time interval to the next, most individuals choose their ideas by copying someone else. A small percentage of the pool of individuals, however, invents something new as opposed to copying an existing idea. Do this over and over, in a series of time steps. It's that simple. If you like, one extra parameter that could be added is "memory," that is, how far back in time someone can copy.

Despite its simplicity, the undirected-copying model is surprisingly powerful. For this it owes much to cascade models. The copying functions act like the interconnections. The minority of new ideas in every time interval (somewhere between about 1 percent and 10 percent of the agents have their own ideas) function like the small triggers in the cascade models—new sand grains, matches dropped, and so on. And just as with the cascade models, a new idea usually doesn't change much, but every once in a while a new idea becomes a big hit, all through the luck of copying.

In fact, models of undirected copying can replicate all the population-scale patterns we have been discussing—long tails, continual flux, and unpredictability—that economists have looked at for over a century. Undirected copying produces long-tail distributions quite naturally, as most new ideas fail and only a few lucky ones become inordinately popular. The model can fit almost perfectly the long tail of baby name popularity, for example. The extra memory parameter gives it more flexibility and makes the model able to replicate the long tails in all sorts of realms, from RSS feed popularity to music sales.

Lots of "rich-get-richer" mathematical models can produce long tails, but their major shortcoming is failing to produce change, or turnover, *within* the long tail—those with less can never overtake those with more. Undirected copying nicely produces this turnover; the more popular a variant is, the more likely it will be copied again, but this is not a fixed rule as in the rich-get-richer models. What sets undirected copying apart is the unpredictability and the continual flux, where the rich may get richer for a while but not forever. The top forty (the exact number is immaterial) is in continual flux.

This resembles the real world, with the constant rising and falling of fortunes everywhere within the long tail, even at the very top, whether we are talking about Fortune 500 companies, city populations, fashion popularity, product sales, or even trendy academic buzzwords. This turnover is often remarkably regular. Among baby names in the United States, for example, there was a consistent average of about four new boys' names and five girls' names entering the respective top-100 lists each year, for nearly the entire twentieth century. Even certain songs of birds show the same kinds of turnover. Chestnut-sided warblers of Massachusetts sing two kinds of songs—one for male courtship of females and the other for competition between males—that are transmitted between birds by learning. Over twenty years, male courtship tunes, under strong selection by females, hardly changed and do not fit the undirected-copying model. Females do not select male competition songs, which frees the males to make new songs out of the copied elements. The competition songs fit the undirected-copying model very well, with a long tail of popularity and continual turnover in the top ten.

Academicians are sometimes like chirping birds. In a certain niche of academic social science, the list of top-five favorite buzzwords turned over by an average of 20 percent a year for over a decade. This means that about one buzzword a year is replaced by a new one in the popular academic lexicon. The hottest words in social theory included "agency" in 1995, "knowledge" in 2002, and "practice" in 2006, all of which (thankfully) are less popular now.

With undirected copying, turnover results from a balance of innovation, which introduces new ideas, and random drift, by which variation is lost through the luck of the draw. New ideas become highly popular by chance alone and then over time become replaced by others, all through drift. The more new ideas, the more they must compete with each other. The two balance out, and so adding more ideas does not necessarily change the turnover of the top forty. Equally counterintuitive, the turnover is fairly constant, no matter how many people are involved. So, for example, when we look at a trendy bandwagon idea in academic research, we see a continual turnover in the ten most popular buzzwords associated with it, even though more and more scholars are jumping on the bandwagon.

Under undirected copying, the change in the fortunes of any one idea is *stochastic*, that is, it is bumpy and nondirectional. This is because the only important feature of each idea is how popular it is at the moment. It could go up or down from there, depending on how many people copy it. Simultaneously, it is competing against all the other variants out there, as is shown below.

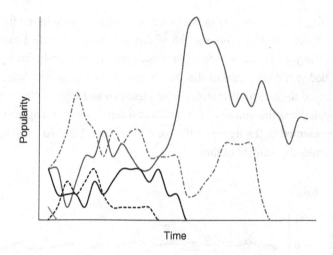

Time

HOW ARE PEOPLE COPYING?

Many people accustomed to more traditional ways of thinking find this kind of rugged, ever-changing landscape, which is so typical of the long-tail world, difficult to navigate. Considering our models of directed versus undirected copying, here are three strategies for helping to make sense of things:

1. Identify what stands out against the background. Undirected copying is often all we can infer at the population scale, but if we zoom in, we can delineate more coherent directions of copying as meaningful departures from the undirected-copying model, as they stand out against it. These can often be seen quite clearly along the lines of variation, flux, and interconnections. In one study, undirected copying served as the background against which to fit data

on dog breed popularity in the twentieth century. Notice in the figure below the rapid rise and fall of dalmatians (filled circles) that
is clearly visible after 1984. The reason for this rise undoubtedly
is tied to the re-release of the Disney movie *101 Dalmatians*. What
enabled the rise in dalmatians to be identified as a case of directed
copying was the null model of undirected copying to test it against,
represented in the figure by the continuous line. Directed copying
changes the element of flux.

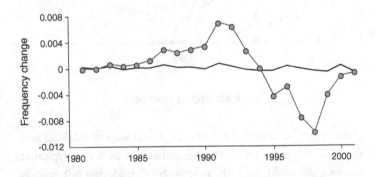

If directed copying is identified against the background, we can
apply the social diffusion models from chapter 3, in which popularity changes smoothly, typically in an S-shaped curve (but sometimes in an *r*-shaped curve). If an idea becomes generally perceived
as better than all others, people's directed, "copy if better" strategy
brings it smoothly into the top forty, where it remains until something better comes along. As long as copying is directed toward the
quality of ideas, then more people means more good ideas can be
discovered, selected, and retained by the population. This was the
basis for our discussion in chapter 3, where we said that the origin

of modern human culture was a result of more people, not necessarily of smarter people. This is also why gatherings of people can sometimes lead to rapid insight, because ideas are selected from the group and fed back to the group to build upon.

2. Focus on the interaction among the agents in your population. In democratic societies, it often is considered ideal to direct people's choices toward the qualities of the options ("copy if better") rather than to other people ("copy the majority"). The privacy of the ballot box is one example, where we hope candidates will be considered objectively (some countries even ban opinion and exit polls during the final stages of elections). We also want to make sure that investment decisions are directed toward the value of those investments and not toward the majority activity, which might be panicked selling, or in an undirected manner, which could point toward behavior even more irrational.

The directedness of decision making at the population level can be altered through interconnections, as certain network structures amplify different patterns of copying. In the figure that follows, adapted from the work of Erez Lieberman and colleagues at Harvard, the two networks on the left favor undirected copying, whereas the two on the right favor directed copying. If we want people to generally follow the "copy if better" rule, hoping that quality gets selected, we might promote the networks on the left. The ideas adopted by the agents on the left are greatly dependent on the agent or agents upstream. This is like the classic marketing model of a few inventors who feed truly novel ideas to the early adopters, who then make things fashionable for everyone else. In any case, if we can characterize the *kind* of network, we will have an edge in understanding whether or not the system promotes the innovation of better ideas.

Few people ←——————→ Many people

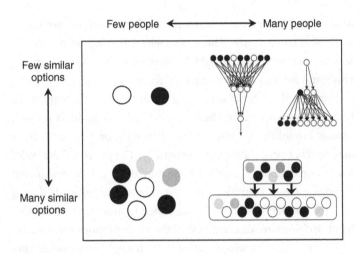

Few similar options

Many similar options

3. Learn to predict and cope with turnover. When all else fails, you can just try better methods of coping with flux and unpredictability. Models of conformity predict little turnover punctuated by massive cascades of change, whereas the undirected-copying model predicts popularity changes fairly continuously. When copying is directed, more innovators probably mean faster change, but if it is undirected, there must be more innovators per capita for turnover to accelerate. If copying is directed toward quality—copying people with true ability or things that are truly better—then there is an evolution toward higher quality.

So what does all of this tell us? It tells us, basically, that undirected copying is often an excellent, population-scale model for our modern long-tail distributions, where flux and unpredictability are often inevitable, no matter how much information we collect. Our financial analyst Jim Cramer had no chance, really, when it came to predicting Bear Stearns. Not only was the financial market a tangled web, saturated with hidden interconnections, but the interconnections were constantly evolving as well. If ideas are essentially copied in an undirected manner, it's better to accept unpredictability and to invest in probabilities, as an insurance company (or gambler) would, rather than expect to predict where things will lead.

MAPPING COLLECTIVE BEHAVIOR

Something odd happened in the upper reaches of the Niger River in West Africa in 1890: a whole mountain range—the soaring Mountains of Kong—disappeared. First charted in 1798 by the English cartographer James Rennell, and appearing on European maps for nearly a century, these mighty mountains—allegedly the source of the Niger itself—just disappeared. Or, to be more precise, they never really existed, having been nothing but a fable. Oddly, when nineteenth-century explorers of the region couldn't locate the mountains, they simply figured they were misreading the maps.

Fictitious places such as the Mountains of Kong acquire reality through social learning, if mapmakers rely on hearsay rather than firsthand experience when they plot geographical features. Even today, phantom locations routinely disappear from Google Maps.

These can be nonexistent streets, such as Torrington Place in East Finchley, London, or even whole towns, such as Argleton in southwestern England, complete with its supposedly world-famous rhubarb factory and castle. Even though they're phantoms, these Google Map locations acquire user-submitted photos and lists of local shopping and services, all through Google's (otherwise remarkable) automated process.

Phantom locations are an inevitable result of a map-making process applied to the wrong scale. Large-scale maps necessarily miss details, and small-scale maps necessarily lack information on their wider world. Imagine trying to tour the Smithsonian Institution's National Air and Space Museum using a map of Washington, D.C., or using the museum map to try to get around the city. Either would be silly, of course, but social science is replete with maps at different scales as well as phantom locations. Behavioral economist Herbert Gintis describes how each of the major social sciences—economics, anthropology, sociology, and psychology—has a different basic assumption, or mental map, regarding human behavior. When anthropologists describe how two captive monkeys compete for a grape, and then use that description to explain consumer markets or national health policy, this is a bit like using a New York City subway map to drive to Arizona.

When appropriately suited to the scale, however, a good map is wonderfully flexible and can even guide people into the unknown. Millennia ago, Polynesian seafarers navigated vast reaches of the Pacific Ocean using the positions of stars, the directions of subtle ocean swells, and the colors of the skies and water. Within a few centuries they colonized a huge triangle of islands from New Zealand in the southwest, to the Hawaiian Islands in the north, to Rapa Nui (Easter Island) in the southeast. Their success was partly a result of a collective ability to create, share, and improve a mental map of the seas—one that suited their immense scale of navigation. Similarly, Australia's Aboriginal foraging communities have embedded a richly detailed map of environmental resources in their collective view of the cosmos.

Humans have a highly refined, flexible social-mapping ability that has allowed them, like Polynesian seafarers, to navigate larger and larger social distances over the millennia, using increasingly sophisticated means of communication. We opened the book by starting with short social distances and looking at how economics, evolutionary psychology, and game theory assume costs and benefits to predict individual behavior. These lenses, focused as they are on the individual scale, are myopic for understanding how ideas spread and evolve in large populations, where the games are social and are played with considerably more complexity. This is especially true as more information is stored in networks of increasingly specialized minds, which themselves are connected to networks of millions of computers.

Just as a psychologist considers the mind rather than individual neurons, in this global, "collective mind" society, we consider populations differently than individuals. Even when individual decisions are defined very simply, their aggregate effects at the population scale can be complex. In a global, communication-saturated society, we navigate out in the rolling social seas, far from the prominent buoys of clear and important options, where copying others is often the best possible strategy. We have introduced a rough but useful distinction between copying that is *directed* in some way versus copying that is *undirected*, at least at the population scale. Determining which predominates in a certain situation becomes crucial in anticipating and preparing for the future.

A MAP WITH FOUR REGIONS

Here we'll attempt to unify the different approaches we've discussed as functions of both the scale of population and the redundancy of choice. We present a conceptual map for navigating from our individual instincts, which evolved in small groups, into the modern age of huge populations and an enormous number of choices. The map's directions are based on how many people are deciding among how many similar choices.

We start with the box presented at the end of chapter 6 and add a compass to turn it into a map with the four cardinal directions. The east-west axis represents the size of the population interacting around a particular behavior. Are we talking about individuals or small groups making their own decisions or about a mass population highly integrated by communication? The north-south axis represents how many *similar* behaviors there are to choose from, or conversely, how easily the person doing the choosing can discriminate among the different options.

This simple map space is not only conceptually helpful but practical, too, because the directions are phenomena that we can quantify, or at least qualify within fairly narrow limits, for different situations. Although the map is meant to represent a continuous space, we consider its four major quadrants.

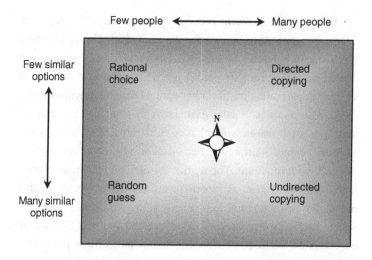

NORTHWEST: INDIVIDUALS CHOOSE FROM DIFFERENT OPTIONS

Much of the traditional conventional wisdom in social science and public policy lies in the northwest quadrant of the map. Rational-actor theories such as classical economics lie squarely in the northwest, where each individual carefully considers the inherent costs and benefits of all options. Behavioral economics is also in this quadrant because it mainly assumes individuals choose independently, but slightly to the east as it also assumes they make humanly imperfect calculations from the information they find. To scale this up to populations, it often is assumed that the "invisible hand" of the market finds the best price or that cultural selection finds the optimal behavior—or at least the one that our brains are wired to prefer—and brings it to the top.

The northwest quadrant is therefore where we find things with clear cost-benefit implications for the individual. The place where we choose to find food, for example, has a travel cost, and this cost-benefit ratio may roughly predict prehistoric hunting patterns or modern supermarket traffic. Other options may be functionally different. Our analysis of sales data shows that the size (but not the brand) of a television, which has to fit the space available, or the category of deodorant application—roll-on versus spray—plots in the northwest quadrant. The market for high-end technology often falls in the northwest, as expert consumers (collectors and audiophiles, for example) tend to be highly selective. Other options are selected strongly on cost alone. A paper-towel business that sells to the industrial sector has buyers who ignore all efforts at packaging, different cuts of tissue, or marketing and ask flatly, "What's the unit price?"

The diagnostic features of the northwest are all familiar: a steady equilibrium (the "invisible hand") and normal (bell-shaped) distributions of popularity within populations. Those distributions are centered on the best cost-benefit option, and they exhibit little change until something better comes along.

SOUTHWEST: INDIVIDUALS CHOOSE FROM MANY SIMILAR OPTIONS

Situations confronted individually but *without* clear solutions populate the southwest quadrant of the map. Importantly, this is different from having ample time and information to carefully comb through many different choices and slowly eliminate inferior options. It is, rather, an individual decision, but one made randomly (often quickly) among many seemingly undifferentiated choices. This may result from lack of information or from an overload of information and no one around to copy. Thus, we just pick an option. Suppose a novice investor turns to a page of the *Wall Street Journal* with hundreds of mutual funds on it—with arcane labels like VHCOX or AWSHX—and, without looking, sticks a pin in the page and buys whatever fund it happens to go through.

With their huge selection, cheap commercial products may lie in the southwest, if there is no social context for making a choice. A college student at the liquor store, looking to get as drunk as possible on four dollars, might contemplate a wall of identically priced boxes of wine or forty-ounce beer bottles. Similarly, a senior citizen who finally decides to get a cell phone will likely be overwhelmed by a whole wall of them, with all their features, pricing plans, and warranties, and think, "Just give me a phone so I can talk to the grandkids!" In each case, if people simply pick one off the wall, their behavior falls in the southwest quadrant.

In making choices, we sometimes use a process of elimination and then pick from the remaining qualified candidates. Increasingly, this is a rich area for commercial exploitation. Think of all those websites designed to make it easier for us to get to a shortlist of options ("compare now"), whether it be related to finance, clothing, or phone apps. The process of elimination could be located in the northwest quadrant ("I want a cheap one!"), but the final action—to just pick one that's left ("So many cheap ones to choose from!")—may be in the southwest. It lies in the southwest if, after narrowing the list, the final decision becomes a random selection from among the qualified alternatives. If, as it turns out, we copy someone else, then it falls in the northeast or southeast, as we'll see in a moment.

For popular media, the data generally reveal that the southwest is not so common. Choosing randomly from qualified alternatives would not produce the long-tail distribution we see among bestselling books, music, and movies, for example. Also, there should be no consistency in the rank-order of popularity from one time period to the next. In the southwest quadrant, the most popular item does not have the inherent advantage gained from people copying each other.

NORTHEAST: INTERACTING POPULATIONS COPY FROM DIFFERENT OPTIONS

In the northeast quadrant, we find what we have called *directed copying* among large numbers of interconnected individuals. Copying could be directed either at certain kinds of people, perhaps relatives or prestigious individuals, or directed toward the majority holding the "received wisdom." Copying the most successful means we have enough information to recognize real talent, such as a small band of hunter-gatherers in which everyone knows who the best hunter is. This is where we can apply the Malcolm Gladwell prescription that genius takes 10,000-plus hours of practice. In the northeast quadrant, such genius won't be wasted.

Copying success can mean copying groups rather than merely copying individuals. As Oded Shenkar describes in *Copycats*, businesses achieve commercial success through ruthlessly directed copying. For example, when White Castle founder Walter Anderson perfected the concept of a fast-food restaurant in 1921, a slew of competitors followed, all following the "copy-the-successful" strategy. Some of them *were* successful, which spawned another generation of copiers, and so on. Similarly, the bow and arrow, once it appeared in the American Midwest 1,400 years ago, spread within a hundred years throughout eastern North America via copying directed toward the better technology and the success of those using it. The copying was not perfect, as an arrow has a shaft, a stone tip, fletching, and lashing, and apprentices inevitably introduced minor differences. Over time, these "copying errors" led to the regionalization of arrow styles across prehistoric North America.

As copying becomes directed toward the majority, conformity fits in the northeast quadrant. Research on conformity dates back to the classic social psychology of the 1950s and 1960s—how quickly conformity creates social norms, when and why people conform, and how we punish those who don't. In the early 1960s, Stanley Milgram famously demonstrated that some people will believe an "expert," even to the point of administering near-lethal electric shocks to a supposed victim. For modern agents of conformity, we need look no further than the ubiquitous Internet popularity lists that allow us to conform with great accuracy by clicking on the most popular videos, news stories, and so on, with every click recalculating popularity.

Similarly, research has examined the influence of prestigious individuals and how this influence evolved in humans. Prestige and reputation are social by definition, being created through the opinions of other people as a sign of quality or ability. The most prestigious, or successful, hunter, for example, often decides where to hunt for the day, although even prestigious hunters make mistakes, as Captain Ahab's crew found out in *Moby Dick*. Because the influence of a few individuals directs the copying of the majority, most who seek prestige must not, by definition, achieve it. Nonetheless, many try, often through shortcuts. Charging a high price, such as several hundred dollars for a new "premium" tequila or a designer fragrance, is a common attempt. Others include "gold premier" customer clubs, pretentious academic jargon, silly wine-tasting adjectives, and other language abuses such as, "If myself or any member of the service team can be of any assistance, please do not hesitate to ask."

Directed copying of objects may be transferred from prestigious personalities associated with them. Even before 2000 BC, commodities of the Indus Valley civilization bore clay seals imprinted with the producer's "brand." Prior to the early 1960s, few people used anything but gin as the basic liquor for a martini, but when James Bond showed a preference for vodka martinis, they became the martini of choice among all age sets.

In contrast, celebrity endorsements, because they are not "authentic," take time and tremendous repetition to create any effect. Authenticity is sought in a character such as James Bond, or the Marlboro Man, but also in products themselves. Take, for example, Sears's Craftsman tools, which come with a lifetime guarantee. What could be more authentic than a hard-working hammer that can be replaced free of charge after fifteen years? Adding to authenticity is a storied history and perhaps a distinct region of origin. These features characterize renowned wines and whiskeys and affect how people experience them. This is especially true of single-malt Scotch whiskies, each coming from a distinct region of Scotland, often from lore-laden small distilleries.

If copying is directed, then, as we saw in chapter 4, we can use traditional social-diffusion analysis developed by historians of technology and commercial analysts. Directed copying introduces coherence to group behavior, as with schools of fish, even though individuals may be copying each other only locally. Better things inevitably become commonplace, but they take time to diffuse smoothly through the relevant population, as people must introduce them to each other.

SOUTHEAST: INTERACTING POPULATIONS CHOOSE FROM AMONG SIMILAR OPTIONS

Undirected copying lies in the southeast quadrant, and it often applies to large, interactive populations confronting many similar options, as we discussed in chapter 6. In such populations, the overall direction of copying is indiscernible, with so many similar choices and so many different individual copying biases that they collectively pattern *as if* they are undirected. Paperback books and pop music are usually in the southeast, especially as people are flooded not only by product choices but also by myriad social influences of recommendations, lists sorted by idiosyncratic means, and so on. Lacking any inherent distinctiveness or any obvious social reputation is how things wind up in the southeast—things such as brand names, hackneyed clichés, getting tattoos, buying products with a gratuitous "eco" label, or using a new font (see the 2007 movie *Helvetica*). All these socially influenced activities have much less meaning now than when they originated. We copy them but without consciously recognizing any distinct benefits or particular social value.

Unpredictability is inherent in the southeast quadrant. Matt Salganik, Peter Dodds, and Duncan Watts demonstrated in a controlled experiment that music-downloading behavior is herdlike and unpredictable when people can see what others are downloading. With many choices and many interacting choosers, works of talent and quality had barely more chance than any other of being selected, unlike in the northeast quadrant. This can seem a lot like conformity, which can also produce marked popularity for one particular choice that need not be better than the alternatives. The difference is that conformity makes the most popular choice even more popular than it would be with undirected copying. Also, undirected copying yields continuous turnover in what is most popular, as long as there is some small flux of novel invention in the system. Conversely, conformity tends to restrain this change, sometimes building up to the breaking point of a massive cascade. Recall Watts's model of local conformity we discussed in chapter 5, where every once in a while, one person's small change in behavior tips the balance for those around him and cascades across the population. If this happens, it is again followed by a period of stasis.

The collective behavior from a model of undirected copying shows the diagnostic patterns from chapter 6—long tail, continual turnover, stochastic change—that can be tested against popularity data. Because success does not last in the southeast quadrant, it pays to move to the northeast quadrant. If something has become popular through the luck of undirected copying, this gain can be consolidated by concocting post-hoc reasons for its success to stick. Coke and Pepsi, for example, famously taste almost identical, but each has its own fiercely devoted community. Since most brands demonstrate the patterns of the southeast, achieving "brand loyalty"—a fortuitous move into the northeast—is the elusive Holy Grail of marketing. Andrew Ehrenberg showed how this "loyalty" correlates with a brand's market share, which fits the southeast quadrant, where popularity is sustained merely through its own inertia.

THE AGE OF "WHAT SHE'S HAVING"

If people agree on anything, it is that the world is changing faster, and apparently in less predictable ways. Just as we feel we are in a routine, and have adapted to the new order of the world, things change again: a bank crisis happens, new buzzwords must be learned, new fashions spring up, and new technologies appear. Time, then, is a crucial scale. Our map for daily behavior (eat, work, and sleep) differs from how behaviors change over the years (more obesity, working online, less sleep) or distant generations (domesti-cating animals, farming intensively, developing enzymes to digest milk). It is the long-term process that explains our anxiety over the short term.

Modern Westerners live in a period of unprecedented choices in which we have turned the idea of individual choice into something akin to a religion. This may stem from human history as a general trend starting many millennia ago in the northwest corner of our map and moving to the southeast, from few, important choices to many, largely interchangeable ones. Eric Beinhocker describes the rapidity with which this explosion of diversity has occurred as a "hundred-million-fold, or eight orders of magnitude difference in the complexity and diversity" since the time of our hunter-gath-erer ancestors a little over 10,000 years ago. As Beinhocker points out, the average New Yorker now has a staggering array of choices.

The Walmart near JFK International Airport, for example, has over 100,000 different items in stock. There are more than 50,000 restaurants in the greater New York City area and over 200 television channels on cable TV. That should be enough choices for anyone, but it seems that we always want more.

Perhaps we could even see the general history of ideas as migrating up and down the east coast of our map. Within each category, there is always the potential for a great idea or new technology that, for a little while, gets placed in the northeast quadrant as the idea spreads across the population through directed copying. Inevitably, people copy the idea with smaller and smaller modifications through time—recall the fractal process we discussed in chapter 5. The fractals/trees concept is more than a metaphor, as the repeated branching and rebranching process creates mathematically definable patterns that help describe long-tail phenomena, cognition, cascade evolution, and social organization.

This treelike representation represents both a unique, complex history at the detailed scale and a more general, recognizable pattern at a broader scale. As so many similar choices accumulate, copying becomes less and less directed, and the niche drifts back toward the southeast. The sequence might be evoked for any fashionable idea—an academic theory that becomes copied by many other scholars to the point of a massive cloud of similarly copied ideas or a trendy fashion that gains so many followers as to become mainstream. A bit of urban slang might be innovated in a particular community (northeast quadrant), such as *skint* for "penniless" in 1980s' London, but if it subsequently gets copied into mass culture, the social distinction is lost and the copying becomes undirected (southeast).

A related, more challenging question is how our choice of *people* has changed through time. On the one hand, the number of people we live among has undeniably increased, as populations grew and became not only more urban but also more globally connected. Given our species's evolution in small groups—on the left side of this two-dimensional space—we may tend to mistake *population* patterns—on the right side—as the outcome of individual or small-group decisions. On the other hand, many of the communication technologies developed over the centuries—urban settlements, postal services, telephones, the Internet—have served to keep our personal worlds clustered and familiar, with fewer acquaintances to connect us to the rest of the world. In terms of our map, these communications may help us parse a world trending toward the southeast quadrant into an interconnected montage of personal worlds in the northeast quadrant.

Clearly in many cases we can still perform directed copying because we know quite a bit about a person's prestige, accomplishments, and relationship to us. Our working environment of hierarchical management is based on this knowledge, and many decisions people make are most strongly affected by friends and family. The interesting question lies in the balance of local influences amid far-reaching networks. A teenager's mother may help her decide whether or not to get a crucial vaccine, but what drives the larger consensus that the vaccine is necessary in the first place? We discuss politics with each other, and many of us vote the way our parents did, but what process chooses the candidates? Ideally, the population should select something for its demonstrable superiority—the "wisdom of crowds" effect—but in reality the result all too often reflects the extraordinary social nature of our species and an ability to learn from each other.

BACK IN THE DELI

This brings us back to where we started in the preface, at Katz's Delicatessen, together with Harry, Sally, and the woman at the next table. Without "I'll have what she's having," our world would be very different. On the one hand, it's likely that it would it be much less populated, as our species succeeded partly through its amazing ability of individuals to learn from each other and thereby spread advances from the distant parts of the human tribe. On the other hand, it would also be much poorer in the sense that we would not have the things that we now have nor the millions of options of contemporary life. Maybe some people see that as a good thing, but we don't. Of course, maybe we say that simply because we have our own creature comforts—Johnny Walker whisky, an iMac, a Mercedes convertible—and we just can't bear the thought of a world that didn't have them.

We hope that now for you as much as for us, it comes as no surprise that social learning is the engine for the spread of culture and human behavior. Yes, individual learning is important—it is the source of innovation—but it is social learning, cloaked in all its different biases—that *diffuses* innovations. Accepting this, we figure that mapping the direction and size of social influence is essential for encouraging certain kinds of behavior or ideas in populations. Otherwise, we cannot hope to judge whether something became popular through its inherent quality, which people have deliberately chosen, or through copying and a run of plain, dumb luck. Without knowing what underlies the status quo, shaping behavior in a population is guesswork.

To classify the broader patterns, we have sketched out the diagnostic models—diffusion, cascades, undirected copying—used to predict the patterns expected on the eastern half of our map, where we have social influence in populations. The models for the western section, especially rational decision theory and behavioral economics, are very well established, but it is the eastern half of the map that we feel deserves more attention.

With good data and some simple analysis, a case study can be plotted on this map, which can be terrifically advantageous. If a behavior or idea is being selected over its alternatives, then it is worth investing in further improvement of that idea or behavior directly. Conversely, if an idea or behavior is diffusing through directed copying, for example, then it makes more sense to think less about the behavior itself and focus instead on the context of social influence. If a variant never really takes off—if it doesn't cascade—then this could be a result of an unfavorable influence network or the thresholds to adoption being too high at certain junctures of the potential cascade. If the behavior is undirected copying, then it might be best to accept unpredictability and to treat the whole problem in terms of probabilities, trying to play with the best odds possible.

The main thing to remember is that, like winds or the weather, social behavior is something we can gauge and adapt to, rather than control. Much of the time, "what she's having" is a very good bet.

BIBLIOGRAPHY

CHAPTER 1

Anderson, Philip W. "More Is Different." *Science* 177 (1972): 393–396.

Barkow, Jerome H., Leda Cosmides, and John Tooby, eds. *The Adapted Mind: Evolutionary Psychology and the Generation of Culture.* New York: Oxford University Press, 1992.

Buchanan, Mark. *The Social Atom.* London: Bloomsbury, 2007.

Dunbar, Robin I. M. "Coevolution of Neocortical Size, Group Size and Language in Humans." *Behavioral and Brain Sciences* 16 (1993): 681–735.

Hauser, Marc D., Noam Chomsky, and William T. Fitch. "The Faculty of Language: What Is It, Who Has It, and How Did It Evolve?" *Science* 298 (2002): 1569–1579.

Hendrie, Colin A., Helena D. Mannion, and Georgina K. Godfrey. "Evidence to Suggest That Nightclubs Function as Human Sexual Display Grounds." *Behaviour* 146 (2009): 1331–1348.

Miller, Geoffrey, Joshua M. Tybur, and Brent D. Jordan. "Ovulatory Cycle Effects on Tip Earnings by Lap Dancers: Economic Evidence for Human Estrus?" *Evolution and Human Behavior* 28 (2007): 375–381.

Penton-Voak, Ian S., and David I. Perrett. "Female Preference for Male Faces Changes Cyclically: Further Evidence." *Evolution and Human Behavior* 21 (2000): 39–48.

Pinker, Steven. *The Blank Slate: The Modern Denial of Human Nature.* New York: Viking, 2002.

Platek, Steven M., and Devendra Singh. "Optimal Waist-to-Hip Ratios in Women Activate Neural Reward Centers in Men." *PLoS ONE* 5 (2010): e9042.

Singh, Devendra. "Adaptive Significance of Female Attractiveness: Role of Waist-to-Hip Ratio." *Journal of Personality and Social Psychology* 65 (1993): 293–307.

Smail, Daniel L. *On Deep History and the Brain.* Berkeley and Los Angeles: University of California Press, 2007.

Yu, Douglas W., and Glenn H. Shepard. "Is Beauty in the Eye of the Beholder?" *Nature* 396 (1998): 321–322.

Zerjal, Tatiana, Yali Xue, Giorgio Bertorelle, et al. "The Genetic Legacy of the Mongols." *American Journal of Human Genetics* 72 (2003): 717–721.

CHAPTER 2

Axelrod, Robert. *The Evolution of Cooperation.* New York: Basic Books, 1984.

Dawkins, Richard. *The Selfish Gene.* Oxford: Oxford University Press, 1976.

Duch, Jordi, Joshua S. Saitzman, and Luís A. Nunes Amaral. "Quantifying the Performance of Individual Players in a Team Activity." *PLoS ONE* 5 (2010): e10937.

Guimerà, Roger, Brian Uzzi, Jarrett Spiro, and Luís A. Nunes Amaral. "Team Assembly Mechanisms Determine Collaboration Network Structure and Team Performance." *Science* 308 (2005): 697–702.

Henrich, Joseph, Robert Boyd, Samuel Bowles, et al. "'Economic Man' in Cross-Cultural Perspective: Behavioral Experiments in 15 Small-Scale Societies." *Behavioral and Brain Sciences* 28 (2005): 795–855.

Holden, Clare J., and Ruth Mace. "Spread of Cattle Pastoralism Led to the Loss of Matriliny in Africa: A Co-evolutionary Analysis." *Proceedings of the Royal Society B: Biological Sciences* 270 (2003): 2425–2433.

Hrdy, Sarah B. *Mothers and Others: The Evolutionary Origins of Mutual Understanding.* Cambridge, Mass.: Harvard University Press, 2009.

Marshall, Lorna J. "The Kin Terminology of the !Kung Bushmen." *Africa* 27 (1957): 1–25.

Nowak, Martin A. *Evolutionary Dynamics: Exploring the Equations of Life.* Cambridge, Mass.: Harvard University Press, 2006.

Nowak, Martin A. "Five Rules for the Evolution of Cooperation." *Science* 314 (2006): 1560–1563.

Schelling, Thomas C. "Dynamic Models of Segregation." *Journal of Mathematical Sociology* 1 (1971): 143–186.

Smith, Jeff, David Van Dyken, and Peter C. Zee. "Generalization of Hamilton's Rule for the Evolution of Microbial Cooperation." *Science* 328 (2010): 1700–1703.

Tomasello, Michael. *Why We Cooperate.* Cambridge, Mass.: MIT Press, 2009.

Wuchty, Stefan, Benjamin F. Jones, and Brian Uzzi. "The Increasing Dominance of Teams in Production of Knowledge." *Science* 316 (2005): 1036–1039.

CHAPTER 3

Aiello, Leslie C., and Robin I. M. Dunbar. "Neocortex Size, Group Size, and the Evolution of Language." *Current Anthropology* 34 (1993): 184–193.

Bass, Frank M. "A New Product Growth Model for Consumer Durables." *Management Science* 15 (1969): 215–227.

Beinhocker, Eric. *The Origin of Wealth: Evolution, Complexity, and the Radical Remaking of Economics.* New York: Random House, 2006.

Bentley, R. Alexander, and Michael J. O'Brien. "The Selectivity of Social Learning and the Tempo of Cultural Evolution." *Journal of Evolutionary Psychology* 9 (2011): 1–17.

Bentley, R. Alexander, and Paul Ormerod. "Tradition and Fashion in Consumer Choice." *Scottish Journal of Political Economy* 56 (2009): 371–381.

Boyd, Robert, and Peter J. Richerson. *Culture and the Evolutionary Process.* Chicago: University of Chicago Press, 1985.

Couzin, Iain. "Collective Minds." *Nature* 445 (2007): 715.

Cronk, Lee, and Andrew Gerkey. "Kinship and Descent." In *The Oxford Handbook of Evolutionary Psychology,* ed. Robin Dunbar and Louise Barrett, 463–478. Oxford: Oxford University Press, 2007.

Dunbar, Robin I. M. "The Social Brain Hypothesis." *Evolutionary Anthropology* 7 (1998): 178–190.

Everett, Daniel. "Cultural Constraints on Grammar and Cognition in Pirahã: Another Look at the Design Features of Human Language." *Current Anthropology* 46 (2005): 621–646.

Griliches, Zvi. "Hybrid Corn: An Exploration in the Economics of Technological Change." *Econometrica* 25 (1957): 501–522.

Hill, Russell A., R. Alexander Bentley, and Robin I. M. Dunbar. "Network Scaling Reveals Consistent Fractal Pattern in Hierarchical Mammalian Societies." *Biology Letters* 4 (2008): 748–751.

Humphrey, Nicholas. "The Social Function of Intellect." In *Growing Points in Ethology*, ed. Paul P. G. Bateson and Robert A. Hinde, 303–317. Cambridge: Cambridge University Press, 1976.

Keynes, John Maynard. "The General Theory of Employment." *Quarterly Review of Economics* 51 (1937): 209–223.

Kovács, Ágnes M., Erno Téglás, and Ansgar D. Endress. "The Social Sense: Susceptibility to Others' Beliefs in Human Infants and Adults." *Science* 330 (2010): 1830–1834.

Laland, Kevin N. "Social Learning Strategies." *Learning & Behavior* 32 (2004): 4–14.

Laland, Kevin N., and Simon M. Reader. "Comparative Perspectives on Human Innovation." In *Innovation in Cultural Systems: Contributions from Evolutionary Anthropology*, ed. Michael J. O'Brien and Stephen J. Shennan, 37–51. Cambridge, Mass.: MIT Press, 2010.

Powell, Adam, Stephen Shennan, and Mark G. Thomas. "Late Pleistocene Demography and the Appearance of Modern Human Behavior." *Science* 324 (2009): 1298–1301.

Richerson, Peter J., and Robert Boyd. *Not by Genes Alone*. Chicago: University of Chicago Press, 2005.

Rizzolatti, Giacomo, Corrado Sinigaglia, and Frances Anderson. *Mirrors in the Brain: How Our Minds Share Actions, Emotions, and Experience*. New York: Oxford University Press, 2008.

Slack, Gordy. "Why We Are Good: Mirror Neurons and the Roots of Empathy." In *The Edge of Reason: Science and Religion in Modern Society*, ed. Alex Bentley, 65–72. London: Continuum Press, 2008.

Surowiecki, James. *The Wisdom of Crowds: Why the Many Are Smarter Than the Few.* London: Abacus, 2005.

Turcotte, Donald L. *Fractals and Chaos in Geology and Geophysics.* Cambridge: Cambridge University Press, 1997.

Whiten, Andrew, Jane Goodall, William C. McGrew, et al. "Cultures in Chimpanzees." *Nature* 399 (1999): 682–685.

Woolley, Anita W., Christopher F. Chabris, Alexander Pentland, Nada Hashmi, and Thomas W. Malone. "Evidence for a Collective Intelligence Factor in the Performance of Human Groups." *Science* 330 (2010): 686–688.

CHAPTER 4

Bentley, R. Alexander, and Paul Ormerod. "A Rapid Method for Assessing Social versus Independent Interest in Health Issues: A Case Study of 'Bird Flu' and 'Swine Flu.'" *Social Science & Medicine* 71 (2009): 482–485.

Berger, Jonah, and Gaël Le Mens. "How Adoption Speed Affects the Abandonment of Cultural Tastes." *Proceedings of the National Academy of Sciences of the United States of America* 106 (2009): 8146–8150.

Couzin, Iain D., Jens Krause, Nigel R. Franks, and Simon A. Levin. "Effective Leadership and Decision-Making in Animal Groups on the Move." *Nature* 433 (2005): 513–516.

Earls, Mark. *Herd: How to Change Mass Behaviour by Harnessing Our True Nature.* New York: Wiley, 2009.

Gladwell Malcolm. "Small Change: Why the Revolution Will Not Be Tweeted." *New Yorker*, October 4, 2010, 68–77.

Kearon, John, and Mark Earls. (2009). "Me-to-We Research: From Asking Unreliable Witnesses about Themselves to Asking People What They Notice, Believe & Predict about Others." In *Proceedings of the European Society for Opinion and Marketing Research Congress*, Montreux, September, 92–111.

Kolbert, Elizabeth. "The Island in the Wind: A Danish Community's Victory over Carbon Emissions." *New Yorker*, July 7, 2008, 68–77.

Michel, Jean-Baptiste, Yuan K. Shen, Aviva P. Aiden, et al. "Quantitative Analysis of Culture Using Millions of Digitized Books." *Science* 331 (2011): 176–182.

Onnela, Jukka-Pekka, and Felix Reed-Tsochas. "Spontaneous Emergence of Social Influence in Online Systems." *Proceedings of the National Academy of Sciences of the United States of America* 107 (2010): 18375–18380.

Orwell, George. "Politics and the English Language." *Horizon* 13 (1946): 252–265.

Panter-Brick, Catherine, Sian E. Clark, Heather Lomas, Margaret Pinder, and Steve W. Lindsay. "Culturally Compelling Strategies for Behaviour Change: A Social Ecology Model and Case Study in Malaria Prevention." *Social Science & Medicine* 62 (2006): 2810–2825.

Pinker, Steven. *The Stuff of Thought: Language as a Window into Human Nature.* New York: Viking Press, 2007.

Smith, Malcolm T., and Donald M. MacRaild. "Nineteenth-Century Population Structure of Ireland and of the Irish in England and Wales: An Analysis by Isonymy." *American Journal of Human Biology* 21 (2009): 283–289.

Stoneburner, Rand L., and Daniel Low-Beer. "Population-Level HIV Declines and Behavioral Risk Avoidance in Uganda." *Science* 304 (2004): 714–718.

Whiten, Andrew, Antoine Spiteri, Victoria Horner, et al. "Transmission of Multiple Traditions within and between Chimpanzee Groups." *Current Biology* 17 (2007): 1038–1043.

CHAPTER 5

Bak, Per. *How Nature Works: The Science of Self-organized Criticality*. New York: Copernicus, 1996.

Bak, Per, and Kim Sneppen. "Punctuated Equilibrium and Criticality in a Simple Model of Evolution." *Physical Review Letters* 71 (1993): 4083–4086.

Centola, Damon. "The Spread of Behavior in an Online Social Network Experiment." *Science* 329 (2010): 1194–1197.

Christakis, Nicholas A., and James H. Fowler. *Connected: The Surprising Power of Our Social Networks and How They Shape Our Lives*. New York: Little, Brown, 2009.

Clauset, Aaron, Cosma R. Shalizi, and Mark E. J. Newman. "Power-Law Distributions in Empirical Data." *SIAM Review* 51 (2009): 661–703.

Gell-Mann, Murray. *The Quark and the Jaguar: Adventures in the Simple and the Complex*. New York: Freeman, 1994.

Gladwell, Malcolm. *The Tipping Point: How Little Things Can Make a Big Difference*. New York: Little, Brown, 2000.

Gould, Stephen J., and Niles Eldredge. "Punctuated Equilibria: The Tempo and Mode of Evolution Reconsidered." *Paleobiology* 3 (1977): 115–151.

Kauffman, Stuart A. *The Origins of Order: Self-organization and Selection in Evolution*. New York: Oxford University Press, 1993.

Kauffman, Stuart A. *Reinventing the Sacred: A New View of Science, Reason, and Religion*. New York: Basic Books, 2008.

Kay, John. *Obliquity: How Our Goals Are Best Pursued Indirectly*. London: Profile, 2010.

Kimura, Motoo. *The Neutral Theory of Molecular Evolution*. Cambridge: Cambridge University Press, 1983.

Malamud, Bruce D., Gleb Morein, and Donald L. Turcotte. "Forest Fires: An Example of Self-Organized Critical Behavior." *Science* 281 (1998): 1840–1842.

Newman, Mark E. J. *Networks: An Introduction*. Oxford: Oxford University Press, 2010.

Roberts, David C., and Donald L. Turcotte. "Fractality and Self-Organized Criticality of Wars." *Fractals* 6 (1998): 351–357.

Van Valen, Leigh. "A New Evolutionary Law." *Evolutionary Theory* 1 (1973): 1–30.

Watts, Duncan J. "A Simple Model of Global Cascades on Random Networks." *Proceedings of the National Academy of Sciences of the United States of America* 99 (2002): 5766–5771.

CHAPTER 6

Axelrod, Robert D., and Michael D. Cohen. *Harnessing Complexity: Organizational Implications of a Scientific Frontier*. New York: Free Press, 1999.

Earls, Mark, and R. Alexander Bentley. "How Ideas Spread." *Research World* (April 2009): 13–17.

Gladwell, Malcolm. *Blink: The Power of Thinking without Thinking*. New York: Little, Brown, 2005.

Goodhardt, Gerald J., Andrew S. C. Ehrenberg, and Christopher Chatfield. "The Dirichlet: A Comprehensive Model of Buying Behaviour." *Journal of the Royal Statistical Society A* 147 (1984): 621–655.

Gould, Stephen J. *Wonderful Life: The Burgess Shale and the Nature of History*. New York: Norton, 1989.

Hahn, Matthew W., and R. Alexander Bentley. "Drift as a Mechanism for Cultural Change: An Example from Baby Names." *Proceedings of the Royal Society B: Biological Sciences* 270 (2003): S1–S4.

Heider, Fritz. "Attitudes and Cognitive Organization." *The Journal of Psychology* 21 (1946): 107–112.

Henrich, Joseph. "Cultural Transmission and the Diffusion of Innovations: Adoption Dynamics Indicate That Biased Cultural Transmission is the Predominate Force in Behavioral Change." *American Anthropologist* 103 (2001): 992–1013.

Henrich, Joseph. "Demography and Cultural Evolution: How Adaptive Cultural Processes Can Produce Maladaptive Losses: The Tasmanian Case." *American Antiquity* 69 (2004): 197–214.

Herzog, Harold A., R. Alexander Bentley, and Matthew W. Hahn. (2004). "Random Drift and Large Shifts in Popularity of Dog Breeds." *Proceedings of the Royal Society B: Biological Sciences* 271: S353–S356.

Ijiri, Yuji, and Herbert A. Simon. "Business Firm Growth and Size." *American Economic Review* 54 (1964): 77–89.

Lieberman, Erez, Christoph Hauert, and Martin A. Nowak. "Evolutionary Dynamics on Graphs." *Nature* 433 (2005): 312–316.

Lieberson, Stanley. *A Matter of Taste: How Names, Fashions, and Culture Change*. New Haven, Conn.: Yale University Press, 2000.

Ormerod, Paul. *Why Most Things Fail: Evolution, Extinction and Economics*. New York: Pantheon, 2005.

Pennisi, Elizabeth. "Cultural Evolution: Conquering by Copying." *Science* 328 (2010): 165–167.

Rendell, Luke, Robert Boyd, Daniel Cownden, et al. "Why Copy Others? Insights from the Social Learning Strategies Tournament." *Science* 328 (2010): 208–213.

CHAPTER 7

Beinhocker, Eric. *The Origin of Wealth: Evolution, Complexity, and the Radical Remaking of Economics*. New York: Random House, 2006.

Boyd, Robert, and Peter J. Richerson. *Culture and the Evolutionary Process*. Chicago: University of Chicago Press, 1985.

Ehrenberg, Andrew. "Even the Social Sciences Have Laws." *Nature* 365 (1993): 385.

Henrich, Joseph, and Robert Boyd. "The Evolution of Conformist Transmission and the Emergence of Between-Group Differences." *Evolution and Human Behavior* 19 (1998): 215–241.

McElreath, Richard, and Robert Boyd. *Mathematical Models of Social Evolution: A Guide for the Perplexed*. Chicago: University of Chicago Press, 2007.

Mesoudi, Alex, and Stephen Lycett. "Random Copying, Frequency-Dependent Copying and Culture Change." *Evolution and Human Behavior* 30 (2009): 41–48.

Milgram, Stanley. "Behavioral Study of Obedience." *Journal of Abnormal and Social Psychology* 67 (1963): 371–378.

Richerson, Peter J., and Robert Boyd. *Not by Genes Alone*. Chicago: University of Chicago Press, 2005.

Salganik, Matthew J., Peter S. Dodds, and Duncan J. Watts. "Experimental Study of Inequality and Unpredictability in an Artificial Cultural Market." *Science* 311 (2006): 854–856.

Shenkar, Oded. *Copycats: How Smart Companies Use Imitation to Gain a Strategic Edge*. Cambridge, Mass.: Harvard Business Press, 2010.

van Vugt, Mark, and Anjana Ahuja. *Why Some People Lead, Why Others Follow, and Why It Matters*. New York: HarperBusiness, 2010.

INDEX

Printed in the United States
by Baker & Taylor Publisher Services